ETHNIC STYLE

CROSS RIVER PRESS
A Division of Abbeville Publishing Group
New York London Paris

TO LEO, WILL AND ROGER

First published in the United States of America in 1992 by Cross River Press, a division of Abbeville Publishing Group, 488 Madison Avenue, New York, NY 10022.
First edition
10 9 8 7 6 5 4

First published in Great Britain in 1991 by Conran Octopus Limited, 37 Shelton Street, London WC2H 9HN

Printed in Hong Kong and bound in China

ISBN 1-55859-368-3

Project Editor: ***Joanna Bradshaw***
Editorial Assistant: ***Rod Mackenzie***
Art Editor: ***Karen Bowen***
Picture Research: ***Jessica Walton***
Production: ***Jackie Kernaghan***

CONTENTS

18 50

INTERNATIONAL ETHNIC

There is more to life than stripped pine. More even than stencils on tastefully colourwashed walls. Around the world, people have responded to the profound human urge to make a home in very different ways: centuries of evolution have led to the spare and elegant Japanese house, whose structure, its very ribcage, is part of its unchanging traditional beauty, and where the decorative impulse is to pare away the inessentials to reach the true identity of the wood, paper and bamboo from which it is built. By contrast South African mud buildings do not share the worthy integrity of the Oriental style but they are an eclectic triumph, taking whimsical bits and pieces from whatever comes to hand, creating baroque and witty pastiches of doughty Edwardian artefacts in materials as ephemeral and eternal as the earth and grasses of which these houses are a transitional stage – this is the opposite process to that which inspires a hoarding of the past, tethering it to the future with conservation, gifts and legacies – this is a way of life that celebrates the moment, making much with nothing.

Ingenuity is what characterizes ethnic thinking, making the most of what you have, stretching and exploiting limited resources, making the solution eclipse the problem – this finds expression in creations as diverse as the plain and sophisticated Shaker cherrywood box where utility

combined with perfectionist technique generates beauty, and at the other extreme the rococo vibrancy of Mexican ceramics, all extraneous twiddles and twirls, irreverently painted, and made from nothing more than glazed earth. Where earth or wood is all you have, they can fulfil many functions and take on a million forms. Similarly with textiles. The primitive backstrap loom is a highly portable and universal means by which cotton or wool can be woven into long narrow strips. Depending on which part of the globe you are inhabiting, these will then be sewn together to create hammocks, sashes, curtains, blankets or rugs. Entire homes or rooms even. In the baking heat of India and North Africa, ephemeral curtains provide all the privacy required and allow breezes to cool those within.

What unites the whole world is colour. Colour costs nothing, textiles can be dyed to brilliant rainbows with berries and roots; syncopated chevrons can dance across walls, fuelled by nothing more than mud. Icy Greek blue and white in combination, the bloom of dusty fruit colours in rural Italy; singing synthetic sweet pinks and yellows in the Caribbean, in vibrant celebration of E numbers – colour is potent magic achieved with the most simple and universal means. Even the subtle traditional colours of Scandinavian woodwork are made with a very basic formula composed of linseed oil and turpentine mixed with easily available dry pigment.

The world divides into two tribes – those who scurry indoors when the snow begins to fall, whose possessions are consolation for long winter evenings – and those who have no winter and for whom the street is an additional and much used room, who habitually work under the vines and just step inside to fetch a basket for the knitting wool, or scissors to cut the embroidery thread. Here the decoration will probably be more exuberant outside than in.

And there are the nomads who have such a passion for open spaces that the whole world is not enough, and for whom home is not a place but a group of people with very few possessions.

It is this fascinating urge to decorate that unites the family of man, where each can enrich the other. Imbenge Zulu baskets for example, swirling cocktails of colour made from telephone wire, speak a common language with the conventional finesse of Chinese bamboo wedding baskets. And the brilliant backstrap woven textiles of Guatemala bear a close relationship to the bright patterned strips that make a hammock in Sierra Leone; the flat-weave kelims of Anatolia have a fraternal resemblance to Navajo rugs and Finnish *ryiji* wedding carpets. The aim of this book is to celebrate the indomitable genius of the human spirit in *all* its variety.

EUROPE

Typical European buildings range from the barn-like, small-windowed clapboard dwellings that characterize the conifer culture in the far north, to the earth and stone houses of the Mediterranean with their brilliant white walls and corrugated terracotta roofs. The further north you go, the more important home becomes as a place of warmth and refuge – summers are poignantly hedonistic and daylight merges imperceptibly into gentle twilight without becoming dark.

But these are passing pleasures paid for by a brumal revenge whose unmitigated cold and dark consigns summer butterflies to indoor confinement. This is one source of cottage industry of the wood-whittling and *rosmalning* variety, and the winter weaving of the eternal multicoloured rag runners. In the south, indoors and out are less aggressively designated, and black-clad women sit and sew under the jagged shadows of vine leaves.

WOODEN ART
With a fluency gained from generations of trial and error, this Finnish interior is quietly elegant, incorporating intricate but unobtrusive carving and a soft harmony of colours on worn, stained and painted wood. The floor is plain, but for the traditional runner.

EMBROIDERY IN WOOD
Top left The simplest of log cabins, embellished with layered frills of fretwork barge-boarding, emerges as a natural and organic extension of the woods in which it stands. Within, the floor is raised and ventilated to prevent the whole building from composting back to its original state, and the weathered birch logs are shaped and right-angled for stability.

CONTROLLED EXCESS
Right A passion for pattern is here held in check by a strict adherence to certain colours: a precisely matched shade of scarlet spattered with strong green and yellow predominates against a calming background of white. The whole composition is held together by a coherence of texture – designs on windows, bed-hangings, and furniture have a similar weight; stripes link up with stripes and floral motifs make visual puns with each other.

Eastern Europe, from the Baltic to the Adriatic and Black Seas, comprising Poland, Czechoslovakia, Hungary, Romania, Yugoslavia, Albania and Bulgaria is an area of cultural overlap, held in a timewarp of poverty, and clamped firmly to history. In some country areas people still live directly off the land, in a way that looks archaic yet idyllic to the city-sick stranger. This is a life of rural simplicity; simple whitewashed houses, occasionally painted with motifs on wood or plaster panels; walls flushed scarlet when covered with strands of drying paprika peppers, and indoors a wild exuberance of textiles, whether brightly woven fabrics, floral printed cotton or dowry embroidery.

In Russia, the wooden architecture is simply magnificent – it relies for its beauty on three-dimensional carving as much as colour, and confident craftsmanship gives disproportionate richness to otherwise very basic buildings. The passion for decoration flaunted in the striped and patterned onion domes of St Basil's cathedral in Moscow, finds sober and eloquent expression in the finely carved lintels and shutters on otherwise humble Siberian log houses. Novgorod is the heartland of extraordinary carved wooden buildings, where its open-air museum boasts houses embellished with flowers, swags, tassels and curlicues – a lively conglomeration of cracked and bleached timber carved according to ancient traditions.

North of Moscow, between Vladimir and Suzdal, are wooden houses built of horizontal tongued-and-grooved timber or solid logs and painted in the most wonderful and subtle greys, olive green, ochre, cinnamon brown and faded blue-green. All the houses are adorned with balconies, decorated pilasters, bargeboarded dormer windows and white-painted, intricately carved window surrounds and shutters. In Rostov, wooden elaboration is taken to even further extremes, and the incredible fretwork of the window surrounds and eaves on peasant houses achieves the delicate effect of embroidery on wood. Mad, but divine.

Behind the lace curtains of a rural Russian house, there is often an unexpected burst of vibrant primary colour; no subtlety here, just a wild exuberance of textiles, embroidered and printed in viridian, ochre and black, on a background of brilliant scarlet. These textiles look

1979

spectacular hung on walls and bring stained-glass brilliance to seats, beds and tables.

In contrast with this almost universal use of wood in Russian rural architecture, there is a tradition for complex and decorative brick, stucco or tile facades in grander buildings. But it was not until the discovery of marble, granite, labradorite, malachite and porphyry in Siberia and the Ukraine in the nineteenth century that a baroque explosion of cathedrals and imperial palaces took place. The characteristic fantastical architecture of gilded onion domes came about when the original Greek and Byzantine religious buildings were changed to suit a hostile climate – windows narrowed, roofs pitched more steeply, and the threat of heavy winter snows led to the evolution of the bulbous pointed dome from its rounded predecessor. With the cosmopolitan tendencies and proselytizing will of Peter the Great, the door opened briefly to European styles and culture.

In the Slovenian Alps, wooden chalets are built to withstand extremes of hot and cold. Houses are completely buried in snow during the winter, but in summer local beaches are ribbed with sun-baked bodies. In Croatia, houses are often built according to the Mediterranean formula of whitewashed plaster topped with terracotta tiled roofs. Or they may be made of compressed earth roofed with reeds; cottages may be built of cob and have an insulating roof of thatch; strange conical shepherd's huts may erupt on the hills; or the houses may be wooden, of complex design with jutting eaves and broad open balconies, filled with fretwork.

There is a less dignified and more folksy flavour in the architecture and artefacts of the Swiss Alps – the same basic approach to using wood as a building material prevails, but with the addition of red-checked gingham and a penchant for heart cutouts in otherwise perfectly acceptable wooden shutters. Alpine villages typically consist of wooden buildings clustered around a commanding white-painted church and belfry. Steeply pitched tiled roofs, which have been evolved to cope with the weight of a winter deluge of snow, overhang and protect generous balconies from which to view the stunning panorama. Breathtaking by snowlight, spangled with flowers in spring, this is original picture-postcard country.

FRAMES
Opposite **An almost Islamic richness of carving and colour surround an extraordinarily ornate corner stove that is complete with a very prettily decorated iconic niche.**
Above left **Strangely mutated classical motifs are set against a three-dimensional patchwork of colour.**
Above right **Ruggedly textured simplicity – a tiny opening framed with a coarse wishbone of white-painted wood.**
Above **Carved and painted wooden window frames from Russia are a compilation of crisply defined geometric shapes against loden green tongued-and-grooved wood.**

GALWAY COTTAGE
Above Rough-textured plaster and thatch in an Irish cottage of the most unadulterated simplicity, undespoiled by the now sad and familiar incursions of grey and white pebbledash. More serious and elevated architecture is reserved for public houses.

GREAT BRITTANY
Opposite Interior as showcase: pale, finely worked wood in beautifully controlled and detailed panels, touches of asymmetry, and a discreet pointing of cornflower blue and cinnabar red enliven an eclectic display of colourful china.

Ireland, Wales and Scotland, parts of northern France and Cornwall have all been shaped by a Celtic past, and the predominantly rain-soaked vagaries of the weather; a twin heritage that gives rise to a preference for a long, low, thick-walled style of architecture.

From without, the chimney is likely to be the most important feature of a Celtic cottage, indicating the priorities within. When bleak rain-raked winter seems to stretch on for ever, unrelieved by the crisp and bracing brilliance of snow, a blazing peat fire takes on a major role. In Scotland and France cold nights traditionally brought bed and fire ever closer, culminating in the seductively cosy box-bed, often screened off with gingham curtains. In Wales, beds in chilly rooms are often covered by a thick patchwork quilt.

But whitewashed or grey pebbledash walls and basic furniture are only half the story. The South of Ireland has the most wild and lyrical outbreaks of pure impossible colour – neat little boxy buildings which throb with an outrageous Caribbean palette of blues, pinks, yellows and purples. The grave painterly qualities of Breton buildings are well-known and respected, pristine single-storey cottages decorated inside with a fastidious collection of objects. In sober Scotland, cottage facades may be made from a surprisingly frivolous mosaic of pebbles, neatly edged with shells round doors and windows and painted white. The Welsh are pre-eminent with wood – the classic, eponymous dresser is the product of a thoughtful and very deliberate artistic temperament.

A journey through France from north to south is one that neatly documents, via a repertoire of subtle stone colours, the progressively warming climate and more relaxed lifestyle that contrasts with northern European austerity. In the north there are the prim cold grey and sharply pitched or hipped slate roofs of Normandy and tidy tile-hung houses in Picardy, then on to the skeletal severity of the tall timbered buildings of Alsace and the crisply chiselled granite blocks of Finistère. Finally the tumbling ochre and terracotta agglomerations of hillside villages in Vaucluse, with their weathered *tuiles-canales* roofs, mark the end of the journey from north to south, with wooden doors covered in cracked and faded paint, sometimes matt chalky periwinkle blue, dove grey, or dusty green.

GRASS ROOFS
Above left **A pair of turf-topped Finnish houses, complete with integral thermal insulation, grow seamlessly out of the landscape. Huge herringbone blocks of stone tether these innocent buildings firmly to their rough, organic surroundings.**

WOODWORKS
Above right **An ingenious use of space – huge and tiny shelves grow out of the walls, while objects hang from the ceiling poles, making both a bedroom and storage area.**

Scandinavia is a land of mountains, fjords and islands, of winter darkness and isolation – though in Lapland in the far north, there is the hedonistic compensation of eleven weeks of sun that does not set at all in summer. Predictably, richly textured wooden architecture predominates here too, painted typically with foxy falun red, dotted with small, white-framed windows and preserved cosily under trim thatched or, particularly in Iceland where there are no trees, green turf roofs growing seamlessly from the hill pasture behind. These are constructed from a covering of birch bark on the roof structure, on which turf is laid, growing thicker with every year. Like the mud walls of Chinese houses, these roofs are a tribute to the insulating power of earth, conserving the warmth within against the sub-zero temperatures and raging gales outside. In Norway, Finland and Sweden, there is no shortage of timber, but the same bitter winter conditions prevail – centuries of expertise have resulted in an artistry with wood that makes it impervious to weather. Log-cabin walls are meticulously matched and notched and the smallest gaps between timbers filled with earth and moss. As in China, the windows are minimal and face south only. In Norway, winter evenings give time for wood-whittling, of exuberant leaf and flower designs to add further élan to painted furniture. Within, there is a feast of subtle decorative painting in warm greys, greens and blues, gold and rust – *rosmalning*, the naive, ornate technique of painting wooden country furniture is an unselfconscious art that offers an antidote to endless winter nights.

Finland has a strong tradition of fine simplicity in objects and buildings – typical are exteriors of tongued-and-grooved timber, whose pin-striped geometry is painted in soft colours such as dove grey or earth green, punctuated by regular milky blue window frames. The final touch of restrained elegance may be a semi-circular window reminiscent of a Georgian fanlight. Everything in this stylish and fastidious country is an *objet d'art*, with the same attention to simplicity and integrity that characterizes Shaker furniture and artefacts.

Danish cottages are small and low, often built from brightly painted plaster held in a grid of square timbering and topped by a sharply pitched thatched roof. Small works of art occur by chance – the muted colours of a painted wood windowframe may form part of a spontaneous still-life when combined with a sweep of snowy patterned lace and a painted wooden candlestick – a simple and satisfying style.

ROUGH FINNISH
Right **The wonderful texture of crudely hewn and patched wood makes for a *faux naïf* artful contrast with a finely matched and displayed collection of indigo and white china. Mysterious culinary accessories in copper and wood provide further interest.**

KARELIAN WOOD
Bottom right **Open-plan living in a Finnish log cabin — the vast interior space emulates bright snowlight, thanks to white flooring in the form of typical strips of rug — a decorative device beloved of the Scandinavians. Hefty wooden furniture gains a certain grace from curves and delicate paint effects, while the walls are made cheerful by bright hangings.**

CUISINE PAYSANNE
Above left **An air of gentle elegance is achieved by means of faded sky-blue paint, a crumbling floor of polished stone, and an elderly *ad hoc* dresser, roughly painted white. A catholic mixture of terracotta and bright painted pottery completes the picture.**

BEDROCKS
Below left **A characteristic feature of much Mediterranean architecture is its incompleteness – and its charm is that this hasty approach does not really matter. A benign climate and possessions pared down to 'plenty of nothing' make for a casual attitude to security. The shingle floor is a fine and original gesture.**

ITALIAN MINIMAL
Right **A cool interior that is an architectural hybrid of a Joan Miró painting and bucolic beast-house. Icy-looking blue tiles reflect a restrained and spartan collection of carefully chosen designer objects.**

Mediterranean countries have certain familiar characteristics – there is a universal common denominator of whitewashed walls and terracotta roof tiles; sometimes external walls may be painted with a rough colourwash of ochre or blue, often fringed with a rough wreath of shade-providing vines. In Italy, there may be crisp and square white architraves, pilasters, classical pediments or circular windows punctuating the most humble facade with a sense of order and regularity. Shutters cut out the midday glare and heat from the dark expanse within. There is often a shiny floor of cool tiles, huge pale roof beams and minimal furniture. There *are* exceptions to the elegant rectangles of Italian vernacular architecture, such as the strange tiled cones of the houses in Fasano, that resemble a small African outcrop, or the Swiss-style balconied Alpine houses of the Dolomites.

In Spain, the Moors left a decorative legacy of interwoven painted motifs on wood, of arches and pierced and lacy metal grilles, kaleidoscopes of brilliant tiles in intricate geometric patterns and plain plaster walls incised with scrolls, leaves and calligraphic designs that are akin to Celtic art in their confident complexity. Spain and Italy boast balconies and windows encrusted with decorative ironwork, massive wooden doors armed with studs and ornate hinges, as well as a tradition for carved wood and bright ceramics. Further west, in Portugal, whole house-fronts are encased in a brilliant armory of patterned tiles, but in Barroso, houses are still built and roofed in huge primeval blocks of stone – a startling contrast with the fine details of more urban architecture.

Greece is the home of sculptural whitewashed dwellings splashed with clear clean colour on doors and windows, and indeed anywhere else that takes the owner's fancy, including bicycles, old oil cans spilling geraniums, and boats. Roofs are shaped with ridged terracotta tiles or domes, or remain uncompromisingly flat. Floors may be patterned out of black and white pebbles and the interior decoration is utterly plain or totally over the top in a multicoloured conglomeration of kitsch bits and pieces. This style is prevalent on the island of Skyros. Coastal Greece is the final resting place of the breeze block, creating a hasty landscape of unfinished rectangles and a skyline that sprouts steel

MAJORCAN KITCHEN
Above A small, cool pantry that exploits the sculptural sinuosities of clay and plaster, and incorporates such essentials as shelves and fretworked food safes in its chunky wall. The walls are white, in true Majorcan style.

BASIC BEDROOM
Opposite Simple living at its most uncluttered – a drift of lace for a door; plain tiles and matting on the floor. The only frivolity is a curly iron bedhead that counterpoints a curly plaster doorframe, creating a simple but sophisticated interior.

'walking sticks' in a rash of half-finished buildings. Not beautiful, but the real decor is in the airy ephemera of vine-shaded balconies.

There are Greek islands where the houses are an exception to the rule of simplicity. In Pirgi, Hios, buildings undergo an artistic process known as *xysta*: black and white or grey and white stripes of geometric designs are etched into the plaster of the whole facade, which, coupled with curly wrought iron balconies and details picked out in sky blue, lime green and aqua, results in an effect that can only be called psychedelic. Elsewhere on the island, the plaster houses are painted in ochres and pastels.

The most extraordinary Greek buildings, which have a distinctly North African feeling are the dovecotes of Tinos – whitewashed towers whose upper half is pierced by triangular ventilations in every permutation of pattern, repeated more discreetly in the local houses.

A passion for plastic has not quite killed off the old traditions, and in Crete huge terracotta containers, *pithoi*, are still fired with vine prunings; Santorini has its carpet-making school, while bright striped textiles are still woven and bed-hangings embroidered in rural villages.

The clichéd Mediterranean interior is composed of cool tiled floors softened perhaps by thin straw matting, curving and uneven white-washed walls, minimal and often uncomfortable furniture, and windows across which shutters can be closed to keep out the sun. The windows may be permanently open and security protected by curly ironwork. Heavy wooden front doors are likely to be silvered and furrowed by the sun's bleaching and desiccation. Outside, the elements are simple but unbeatable – flat-roofed rectangular houses painted brilliant white, breezy porches and terraces, arched doorways, the shade of ancient olive trees, white, pink and magenta bougainvillea and oleander, aromatic herbs and the resinous scent of pines.

In Andalusia, the typical architecture is composed of white walls, terracotta roof tiles and patios. Walled farmhouses the size of small villages known as *cortijos* dot the dry ochre landscape. On the island of Fuerteventura there are strange carvings on doors and windows in the shape of serpents, suns, plume-crowned heads and pumas, which have an uncanny similarity to

Aztec motifs. Minorca is misty heathland and wind-warped trees – but for the sun and the brilliant whitewashed buildings, you might think you were in Cornwall. On the island of Ibiza the cottages or *casaments* have a strong flavour of Africa about them, with their clusters of white cubic rooms and shady arched porches, and the convoluted village alleys reminiscent of the *souk* (market). Outside is where black-clad women sit and sew; men in shirt-sleeves loll and comment on the local talent; children stare at passers-by. On summer nights doors and windows are open, and the newly acquired and proudly displayed television has sole possession of the interior, while the family sits out in the cool, looking in.

In Spain, Moorish influence was strong but localized. From them came the horseshoe-shaped arch, ornamental relief brickwork, and a passion for decoration which, with the urge to represent people or animals thwarted by the edict of the Koran, found expression in calligraphy, interlaced geometry and elegant stylized plants. Later with the construction of Seville in the twelfth and thirteenth centuries, came the bright glazed tiles or *azulejos* in geometric patterns, their colours separated by strips of manganese. Subsequently pointed arches prevailed over the horseshoe, lobed arches became more elaborate, and doors and windows were emphasized with lacy stonework, paint or tiles.

Dark, Jacobean-looking carved wooden furniture is much loved by the Spaniards, as are elaborate marquetry and hefty wooden chests, which may be strengthened and decorated with bands of ironwork or chased steel, or covered in the embossed and dyed leather originating in Córdoba. Fine wrought iron and metalwork is a historic talent, manifesting itself in delicate window grilles and lacy balconies.

Tiles and ceramics are still made with unselfconscious panache, though lacking the intricate splendour that they once had – from Castille, the Canaries and the Balearic Islands come free-hand painted terracotta pots, casually decked with bright primary bands and patterns. Majolica – characterized by clear base colours and tin glazing – took its name from Majorca but has been somewhat overtaken by vigorous and naive rustic pottery, while Castille is the source of bold blue and yellow *talavera* ware.

BLUE AND WHITE AND GREEK

Left Cerulean blue has a cooling influence on the rasping sun of a Greek summer. The whitewashed plaster has a masculine rough-hewn look, to which the graphic shapes of the painted woodwork make a crisp contrast. This is not exquisite workmanship, but there is a fine confidence with colour and form here – transforming doors, shutters, gates and steps to bold abstract patterns against the prevailing sunbaked white background.

ITALIAN LINES

Right A midday terrace is lined with the stripes of shadows cast by a bamboo awning. Blue and white has the usual magical effect of transforming heat and dust into a cool aqueous landscape nicely partnered here by a steamer chair, a fine web of lace, and a basket or two. The blues of wall, floor and upholstery are skilfully matched and perfectly complemented by the warmth of wood and straw.

AFRICA

Eclectic and ingenious – in Africa things are not necessarily what they seem, and necessity, or humour, is the mother of invention. Given that this is a continent that suffers terrible disasters, and that nature is as cruel in some ways as it is generous in others, there seems to be a contrary determination from the people to make the best of things, and to enjoy doing so. Life is lived in gregarious fashion, out of doors, on the street – people like to congregate, and talk to each other loudly and emphatically.

Architecturally, Africa may make you think of mud huts – and there you may think the matter rests – but there are as many different styles of mud house as there are tribes. Ideas are passed from one region to another, culminating in some places in a style of building which is sophisticated, functional, economical and beautiful. This is sculpture to live in, bare and basic maybe, but far from primitive.

PLATONIC PLUMBING
A tiny stage set for the proper adulation of water – only the taps betray the fact that this is not an altar to a higher deity. Rich raw pumpkin orange walls, brass and panelled wood bordered with studded leather evoke attar of roses and Sheik ablutions.

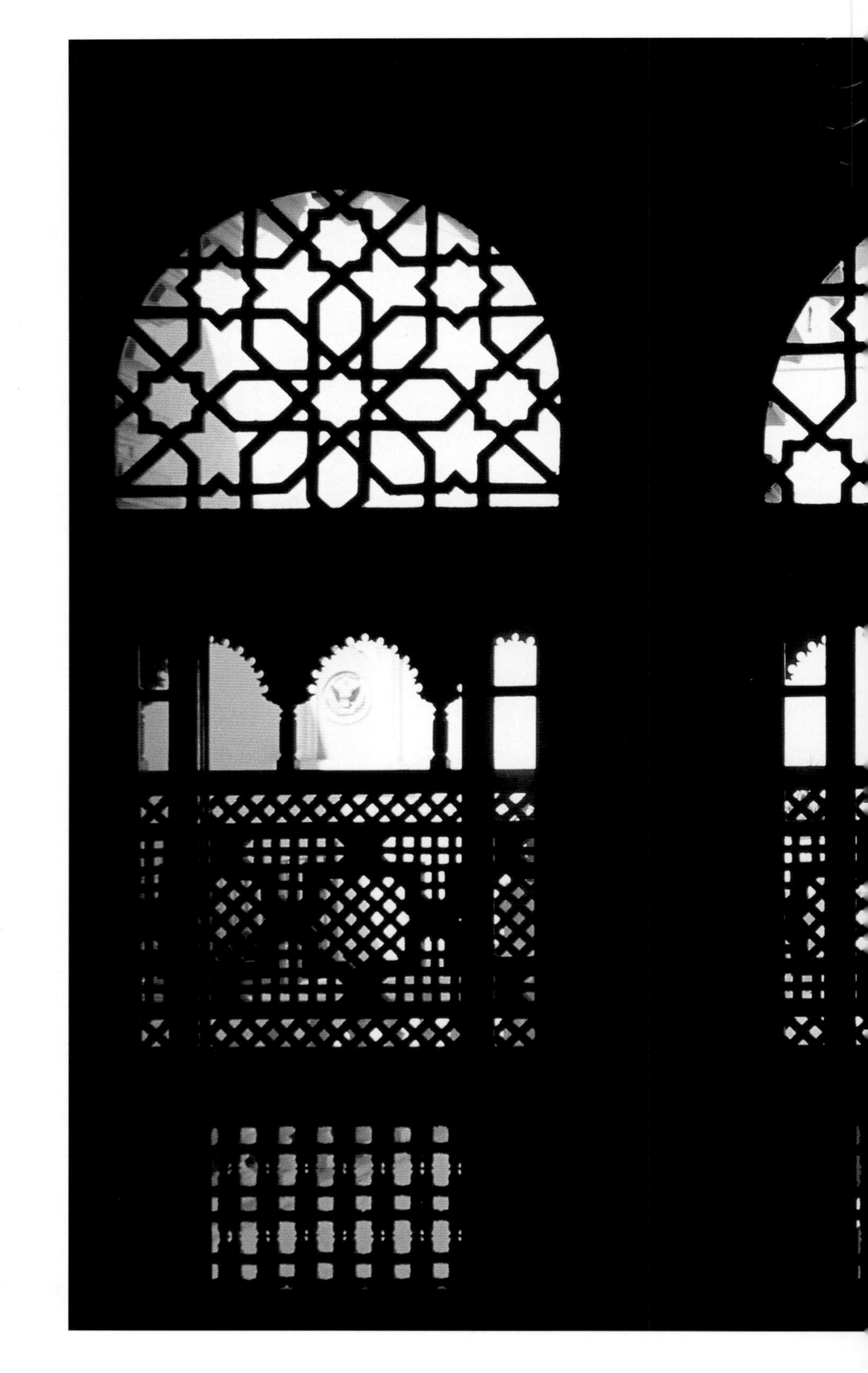

The advantages of mud as a building material include its cheapness and availability, together with its thermal insulation properties – generous thick walls provide warmth in the cold season and resistance to heat in high summer. Mud-built houses also have a sympathy with their environment and are user-friendly.

The peoples of Africa have to contend with wildly differing climates and geography. The Sub Sahara regions undergo violent extremes of heat and cold, allied with less than 100mm (4in) of rain annually, while the Zaire Basin has to cope with 4000mm (160in) of rain annually. Consequently there are many different ways of staying alive, reflected in the buildings. Some tribes are traditionally nomadic, and their dwellings are easily disassembled tents, transportable by camel; others tend long-term assets such as the oil palm, which may endure for a century, and therefore live in much more permanent housing. In between are the people who grow crops like the raffia palm, which last for five years or so, after which the people move on and cultivate a new part of the forest. Where the night-time temperature plummets to near-freezing, mud beds are built to span fireplaces, providing integral central heating.

So, in this world where architectural ambition is necessarily limited to what is locally to hand, what sort of houses do people build?

MARRAKESH ELECTRIC

Far left Brilliant North African sun brings glowing life to an intense blue wall that is etched with the shadows of jasmine-covered trellis. A whimsical filigree 'security sculpture' allows a breeze to flow through open windows.

GEOMETRIC SILHOUETTE

Left Mathematical Moorish interlaced designs offer a decorative device that combines privacy, security, and as much air movement as possible. In a society both gregarious and rule-bound, it also means that women can invisibly observe the world outside. The endless knot of interwoven motifs is akin to Celtic decoration on the same theme.

In the north, in Morocco, *adobe* – unbaked earth bricks – are left out in the sun to dry and harden, and this is the prevalent building material; it generates buildings which are rectangular, sometimes turreted, with a delicate pattern of perforations in the mud with which they are rendered. In the gorges of the Dades valley, tall rust-coloured houses exactly match the earth from which they grew, and similarly in the Dra valley, chocolate-coloured houses, with white bordered windows, stand out in precise geometric relief against a range of ragged chocolate-coloured mountains. Within, there may be tactile rounded pillars metamorphosing effortlessly into seating, or complex notches and indents at ceiling height making a decorative border to a rooflight.

In Algeria, the surface of the red buildings is sometimes faced with bun-shaped handfuls of earth, giving a bubbly texture to walls.

From the outside, North African houses are discreet, with an expanse of ground-floor wall punctuated by small barred windows, a corbelled wooden projection above of intricate lacy carved shutters, and possibly a decorated doorway, above whose arch may be painted a fish or the hand of Fatima (Muhammed's daughter), horns, a cross or a solar rosette – all protective icons to keep the evil eye away from the door. But cross the threshold from the dusty street, and you are greeted by a small sensory paradise – a befountained and tile-decked courtyard, potted citrus trees, and seductive shady rooms, with floor and seating covered in rich garnet red rugs, and the odd sprinkling of chased brass in the form of tables and lamps.

Further south, the walls and doorways of Mauritanian houses are decorated by the women with strong, swirling designs on walls and around doorways – designs which are sometimes first marked on the clay in low relief, whitewashed, and then outlined using a finger dipped in dark red earth pigment. Sometimes they are built up in three dimensions on a plain whitewashed building. House walls are very thick, and cool painted alcoves with built-in seats in the walls surround internal courtyards and provide welcome shade and privacy. Nothing is quite straight in this architecture, and walls, windows and doorways curve with a sinuous attempt at the rectangular.

BEAUTIFUL UTILITY
Opposite A rich display of materials and objects is held together by related pattern and colour. In this Marrakesh house, internal walls incorporate panels of pierced grilles that display a geometry reminiscent of primitive textile designs. Startling chevrons and diamonds on the walls are an addition of the present owner. The overall effect demonstrates the Moorish principle of turning practical problems into beautiful solutions.

FRETWORK BALCONY
Above At Massawa, on the Red Sea, an elaborate carved and turned wooden balcony cantilevered over the street makes the most of any breath of air. There is an appealing irregularity about the facade of this building, an architectural relic of Turkish occupation.

In Cameroon, a traditional solution to the annual summer deluge is a rounded conical skep-shaped mud hut, named a *case-obus* or 'shell-shaped hut' by the French.

Similarly in Senegal, round thatched huts with wide eaves walled with mud or wattle, can withstand heavy monsoon rainfall. Here also some thatched houses are designed with a central well into which rain drains like a giant funnel, as insurance against the dry season. Everywhere there is an obvious homogeneity in mud walls and clay cooking pots. A more modern version of this surprisingly efficient method of housing is in the form of a half-timbered bungalow, with mud and wattle infill between wooden uprights, topped by a hipped roof of neatly finished corrugated iron. Of course, there are more urbane alternatives to this kind of life – thick-walled conventional houses of simple sophistication, painted white or terracotta, with finely striped matting on the floor, low seating either of hardwood or built into the walls, and panelled doors painted olive or periwinkle-blue which may be hung with bright printed or indigo dyed cloth. Socializing tends to go on at floor level, people lounging with apparent comfort on mats on the packed earth. On the other hand, in less refined surroundings, walls may be painted geranium scarlet, with canary-yellow woodwork and a bright turquoise door curtain.

In the Upper Volta, walls are a patchwork of different coloured rectangles – all the rust, cream and chocolate colours of earth; or they may be painted ice-cream pink, superficially incised with diamonds, and punctuated by life-like sculpted geckos. Inside, some of these buildings once had soaring corrugated arches, invisibly reinforced with palm fronds. This type of housing has tragically been 'modernized' out of existence, as have so many of these beautiful, but all too biodegradable, African buildings.

Ghanaian houses have a gingerbread-house quality, with steeply pitched thatched roofs topping small rectangular buildings. The thatch is tidily assembled with horizontal bands of trimming, and the ochre and russet walls are decorated with raised patterns of swirls and tendrils. Alternatively, they may have almost life-size figures of people moulded on to the exterior, or a vast stylized lizard, a protective talisman, twice as tall as a man.

CAREFUL COLOUR
Opposite **A tiny bedroom in Marrakesh is dominated by a baroque brass bed while every decorative detail is linked by a punctilious use of colour. Cream, polished brass and dusty cinnabar dominate. The ribbed, barrel-vaulted ceiling lends an illusion of airiness, the kaleidoscopic *oeil de boeuf* (bull's eye window) and intricate metal filigree work on the ceiling lamp are typical of North Africa.**

PATTERN PATCHWORK
Above **Here the common denominator is a richness of texture: everything is patterned, none of it matches, yet the overall impression is one of harmony. The arched wooden doorframe is designed to cast a graceful silhouette when open.**

A LIGHT SHOWER
Right **An arched shower space, built into thick Moroccan stone walls, is lit by spotlights of yellow glass.**

In South Africa, the Zulus build fine, domed reed houses, lashed together with a highly decorative web of ropes. Doorways are a carefully finished and sophisticated exploitation of a very basic material, worked in concentric ribs of ridged basketwork. Or houses may be firmly constructed domes of pliable bamboo, thatched in ridges like an armadillo's shell, the whole village erupting from the plain like so many bubbles on a simmering pan.

In the Transvaal, the uprooted Ndebele tribe have had to forsake their utterly extraordinary traditional painted houses to live in corrugated iron shacks in an arbitrarily assigned semi-desert 'homeland'. Because the Africans retain a need to decorate their homes, even these pathetic constructions of motley cast-off planks of wood, tin and cardboard have a certain slight beauty – in their neatness, their colours of earth and rust, their carefully smoothed and rounded mud foundations, their general attempt at pride of place. But the contrast with the glorious buildings of their recent past is iniquitous. The traditional houses are simple rectangular barn-shapes with thatched roofs. These are contained in private low-walled courtyards with ornate entrance porticos (an appealing solution to the twin desires for sociability and

defensible space), and are masterpieces of vigorous decorative art – every available wall is painted in a brilliant kaleidoscope of subtle and bright colour, with strong abstract shapes, sharply outlined in black on a white background. Eat your heart out, Piet Mondrian.

The houses of the semi-nomadic Bantu occur in unexpected clumps in the middle of nowhere. Built from wattle and daub of mud and cow-dung or sun-dried earth bricks, they are decorated by the women with competitive zeal. The tools are utterly basic – fingers to mould the clay, trowels, toothbrushes, cardboard stencils coloured with earth and mineral pigment, with the surprising addition of laundry blue applied with rags or fingers. The rippling relief patterns combed with a kitchen fork, or Aztec-looking geometry or ebullient flowers in black, charcoal and sienna sometimes have to be renewed every year after the annual rains have obliterated the design from the walls.

These are transitory places anyway, and there is a humorous eclecticism about their design. The walls may have the additional embellishment of a prized *objet trouvé* – a particularly attractive oil can sprouting a spiky succulent, a pattern of hubcaps pressed into mud walls, or a car number plate. The wall paint-

FRIEZE FRAMED
Far left Fluent but casual decoration in the form of a border has been applied with paint drawn on an otherwise unadorned wall in Sotho.

EARTHWORKS
Confident runic shapes have been applied to a house in decorative celebration.

PRIZE PLATES
Above right The inventive ladies of South Africa can achieve miracles with a lump of clay, a frill of cardboard and three spoons. In this case the wide, bright clay dresser rather outshines the enamel display upon it.

ings are sometimes swirling patterns or ziggurats, of paint; sometimes there is a symbolic component of dots and fish signifying fertility and plenty, lizards or geckoes which are ever-vigilant and protective – the decoration in itself is done as a celebration of the woman's fertility. There is nothing in the world to equal the exuberance and unselfconscious artistry of these houses, and quite apart from the outrage to humanity of obliging people to live in coops, the loss of this fountain of talent would be grievous.

Doorways and windows, though ornately painted, decoratively spiked with porcupine quills, inlaid with coloured pebbles or ribbed with patterns in relief, are often very small – partly to keep out the sun and any itinerant evil spirit, and partly to instil in whoever enters a proper feeling of humility as they stoop to cross the threshold. The furniture inside is minimal, sometimes consisting entirely of a stove and a bench moulded out of mud, on which people sit and sleep. The floor is usually a mixture of mud and cow- or goat-dung, smoothed and polished with pebbles and by constant use. Occasionally, the floor will be corrugated with fine arabesques made with a fork while the surface is damp, and people may run to the luxury of linoleum.

The interiors often sport a witty and ingenious pastiche of the Welsh dresser groaning beneath a display of Spode – but in this case the shelves grow from the wall, created from the tactile puddled mud and cow-dung mixture itself, and edged with cardboard and clay borders simulating the paper frills and oilcloth shelf liners that once adorned the pantry shelves in every self-respecting middle-class home. Again, ingenious Sotho women make use of whatever is to hand in these baroque confections – egg-box crenellations and borders of gathered doilies may enhance a still-life display of Chinese enamel plates and bowls, spoons and light bulbs.

The heritage of indigenous African architecture is a unique and precious one, but one that is peculiarly vulnerable to time, change and decay. Cement and corrugated iron are now cheap and universally available, and in Africa they become part of the repertoire that includes the ubiquitous passion to decorate. But it would be a tragedy to lose completely these beautiful, economical and rational building methods evolved by, and forming part of, the *genius loci*.

FREE STYLE
Opposite Effortless South African magic – creating something from nothing. Walls, floor, shelves, seating, paint – all demonstrate the virtues of mud. Oilcloth and enamel are simply the icing on the cake.

DOORLESS
Top right When you have nothing to lose but your spoons, you can dispense with mortice and deadlock. Extrovert chevrons frame a view of a sunbaked courtyard.

FEATS OF CLAY
Bottom right The rich browns of raw and baked earth form a design of which Klee would have been proud. More spoons hang from integral clay loops beneath the family portraits.

INDIA

The Indian sub-continent encompasses the wooden Alpine villages of the Himalayas with their long snowy winters, the parched heartland of the Great Plain, the lush fertile valleys of the Rivers Indus and Ganges, the monsoons and deserts of the southwest and, at the southernmost tip, Sri Lanka, a textbook tropical paradise.

India is the land of the senses – pulsating colour greets you at every turn and the air is heavy with the fragrance of frangipani, spices and the smells of humanity. Sound, touch and taste all co-exist in glorious excess; it is a rich mixture which excites a strong response – pleasure and dismay in equal measure.

The sub-continent is like an extravagant stage set. Colour adorns everything, from gold embroidered silk upholstery to tattered hangings, all glittering defiantly with mirror insets intended to deflect the evil eye.

DOUBLE CREAM
A wonderfully cool and refreshing antidote to the hectic colour, heat and general chaos of urban India, this peaceful bedroom is brightened only by a small brass ensemble, and clad only in mosquito-proof wafts of cotton. The lobed arch has all the more significance for the simplicity of its setting.

NICHE WORK

Top left **This beautiful, unecological door – a wanton extravagance of ebony and ivory – marks the entrance to a maharani's palace in Udaipur. Stylized flowers, an intricate ceramic surround, brass fittings, and an impossible, bite-shaped arch are typical of India.**

Top centre **In Shekhavati, this haphazard stab at symmetry in architecture and paint, is charming despite its waywardness. Similarly, there is an attempt to achieve a geometrical unity in the painted design that is overwhelmed by the effervescence of calligraphic flowers and *trompe l'oeil* fakery. The muted colours are earthy, rich and subtle.**

Top right **A bold, polychrome version of the painted niche in Shekhavati, India. The richness of the assemblage belies the naivety of the elements and one could profitably reproduce any single motif as a wall or border design, or alternatively put them all together as in the original – to surround a door perhaps.**

ARCH WAYS
Bottom left **Bright Indian pink of unconvincing intensity – made real only by the brooding pigeon. Fancy wood and plaster are lent cohesion by the simple device of a white surround.**

Centre left
Extravagant mirror and tile work in Udaipur. The archway holds a handful of curiously anachronistic Delft and Biblical tiles; an insouciant mixture that is bound together by the predominant strong blue colour.

Bottom right **Flowers and leaves in a disciplined embrace produce a geometry that follows the architectural detail and makes a glorious frame for a pair of religious medallions.**

In Indian architecture, every exterior detail has a symbolic meaning and its inherent decorative richness has evolved over centuries. The stonemason who chisels sandstone to make the 'frozen lace' exterior decoration found in Rajasthan and Gujarat has at the back of his mind an ancient edict. Taken from the pre-Christian Sanskrit Manasara and Shilpshastras, it states that every pedestal must have 24 parts, of which the plinth forms five, the fillet one, the dado 12, the next fillet one, the patica four and the final fillet one. There are rules governing every exterior detail; a subliminal discipline which informs the intuition with a feeling of homogeneity.

Throughout India, sumptuously decorated arched entrances are the aspiration – doors are bordered and painted and the surrounding stucco incised with sinuous flowers picked out in brilliant or subtle colours. Elsewhere they are edged with a casual lapidary patchwork of tiles, which looks Islamic in its richness of design and colour. Alternatively, door surrounds may be made of pressed terracotta in a three-dimensional design of leaves and trees. A doorway may be formed from a kaleidoscopic collection of materials – moulded plaster, painted carved stucco, mirrors and tiles. And to emphasize still further this important and symbolic architectural feature, a temporary punctuation may be added in the form of textiles – the most important doors of a house may be hung with a bright embroidered frieze or *toran*, echoed by *pantorans* to embellish walls, and *pachitpati* hanging from shelves – inset with mirror fragments or finished with tassels.

Interiors may be furnished with integral *sangiras* (food stores) and *kothas* (grain cupboards) built with a mixture of whitewashed mud and cow-dung, or papier mâché. The floor is most often of tamped earth, worn smooth and patinated with use and covered with dhurries.

Glittering ephemera is prized, the walls sparkle with mirrored textiles and mountains of shining copper pots are proudly displayed. Reflective surfaces and shiny fabrics keep the evil eye away. Metal and lurex thread often add their mutating reflections, to hostile-looking brocade bedspreads for example, imparting the sense of a polychrome suit of armour. The beds themselves may stand on improbably tall legs or hang on elaborate chains from the ceiling.

CORRIDOR COURTYARD
Top left **A tiny balcony and staircase achieve undue architectural importance because of their partnership of singing colour. The unpretentious courtyard below gains added dignity from this vibrant colour scheme. Peach, mahogany and aqua are three colours that one might not put together normally; but the combination of tones produces an aged quality that works.**

COOL BLUE KITCHEN
Bottom left **Walls have a plastic quality in India, and are moulded and perforated as if they were as malleable as Plasticine. Here, stone grey and a chill blue create welcome shadows in an overheated climate.**

A PUBLIC FUNCTION
Right **An airy cloister bedroom which opens on to an inner courtyard in Jhunjhunu, in the north of Rajasthan. Elaborate blue and terracotta paintwork and carving on pillars and arches contrasts strangely with the frugality of the possessions displayed in the niches. A single lamp provides light.**

In India there is little evidence of the normal fierce demarcation between indoors and outside. Single-storey houses known as *bangla* (bungalows) may include windows which have a decorative fretwork of wrought iron, but there will probably be no glass therein. The doors and windows of courtyard houses will usually be open both day and night, verandahs will be shaded from the sun and the world by ephemeral *cheeks* – slender curtains of bamboo.

Furniture is movable and sparse – India has been called the land that has no furniture. Beds consist of a thin mattress which can be rolled up and stored out of sight at sunrise; in the summer, *charpoys* may be taken out to the roof or balcony where people sleep under a ceiling of stars; tables and chairs are unnecessary for meals, which will very likely be eaten while sitting on dhurries on the floor. Possessions are stored in simple boxes and chests or tin suitcases painted with birds and flowers.

The walls will not be a showcase for framed paintings – they may very well be paintings themselves. The ubiquitous elephant may take the form of architectural emphasis – with the graceful curve of the head and trunk painted to form a balustrade. Nathdwara is where the traditional, and originally religious wall paintings on handspun cloth known as *pichwais* are made, showing an idyllic verdant scene patrolled by peacocks and parrots (signifying love) where Krishna and Radha disport, brilliant with indigo, cochineal, lapis and orpiment.

In Shekhavati, the houses known as *havelis* – (enclosed space) built round a courtyard, as opposed to *kothis*, or countrified garden houses – are entirely decorated with murals of elephants (bringing power, knowledge and good fortune) or huntsmen, or mythological scenes. In Jaisalmer where rain rarely falls, flat-roofed white houses are decorated with paintings, and doors and windows are outlined with ochre and brown, patterned with trees and peacocks and stylized mango leaves. Heavy wooden doors have a vigorous *ad hoc* quality in which the character of the original tree is still very apparent. In the south, in Cochin, ephemeral houses of woven palm leaves exploit the natural colour and texture of a very simple material – the result has all the airy charm and careful workmanship of a beautifully made basket.

COOL EXTERIOR
Above **A cool simple bed placed beneath breezy open windows looking on to a courtyard. A decorative grille provides security.**

POINTS OF COLOUR
Above right **A jewel-like *pointilliste* stained glass window in Fort D'Amber, Rajastan, surrounded by a richly patterned, unrelated plaster frame.**

FRAMED VIEW
Opposite **A tiny courtyard whose stark furnishings have a calming sufficiency about them – in strong sunlight, even the shadows are decorative.**

In the north, Rajasthan is a state in which the arid desert with its sparse population is tempered by the exuberant dress and decoration of the inhabitants. Men and women in this pale and dusty landscape exult in a riotous array of brilliant textiles and glittering jewellery, and their houses are often decked with beautifully intricate and ornate technicolour murals. In a country where you cannot just nip to the local store for the necessities of life, where collecting a pot of water may involve a walk of several miles, the necessary trips to distant fairs and *hats* (occasional markets) become something of a social event, almost a carnival in some places.

Despite the inhospitable climate and geography, most of the population makes a living from the land. The most common type of farming is sheep, goats, camels and varieties of cattle that have been specially bred to cope with the dry heat. Nearly half of India's wool comes from the state of Rajasthan.

And everything is celebrated with bright and gaudy colour. At the highest level in interior decoration, it finds expression in the exquisite refinement of Udaipur miniature painting – tiny, highly-detailed mythological and domestic scenes painted in clear luminous colour. At a more accessible level there is pure psychedelic kitsch in gaudy packaging and posters.

Rajasthan, as far as textiles are concerned, is known for its outstandingly beautiful fabric dyes and designs. Here, the colour of a sari or a turban is a visible pedigree, a key to caste and religion. In some areas, virtuoso dyers can waft warring primary colours on each side of a piece of cloth with such mastery that neither is aware of the other. In Kota, the lively, shimmering cloth is a result of differently-dyed warp and weft.

Where fabric and pattern carries the burden of so much of the joy in life, every aspect of each element is carefully considered, and every design has meaning. The colours of Rajasthan textiles derive much of their subtlety from earth and vegetable dyes extracted from flowers, bark, roots and minerals: oranges and yellows come from jasmine, myrobalan, and saffron; blue from indigo; green from pistachio; red and purple from mulberry bark and a cochineal-like insect; and black from sulphate of iron. Dyeing was a fine art a century ago – the dyer had 250 colours at his disposal, and when all else failed, ingenuity provided solutions such as a particular green derived from the baize taken from exported English billiard tables.

ASIA AND OCEANIA

Asia and Oceania offer an abundance of traditional decorative effects that are unfamiliar but utterly inspiring. The pristine perfectionism of Japanese interiors with their spotless mats, screens, unpainted wood and paper successfully demonstrate that less is most definitely more. Elsewhere, the instant charisma of brilliant textiles among the Himalayan mountain wanderers never fails to take the breath away; while beautifully crafted Indonesian thatch and bamboo houses are as finely wrought and detailed as a piece of jewellery. These offer a wildly contrasting look from the cheerful *ad hoc* arrangements of rough timber, corrugated iron and bright paint favoured in Australia, where the sun shines dependably and the living is easy. Climate is everything and rain, or the lack of it, temperate warmth, or seasonal extremes of freezing cold and searing heat, affects every aspect of life in these parts of the world.

EMBLEMS OF ASIA
Almost an excess of richness, an overdose of colour and pattern. Every inch of this Thai interior is embellished with paint or gilding, embroidery or carving. But the careful choice of colours – slate blue, lacquer red and gleaming gold – holds the elements together, and achieves a sumptuous look.

By contrast to the hectic richness of India, Japanese houses are characterized by severe simplicity. Steep pitched roofs with overhanging eaves, to withstand heavy snow as well as rain, are common and there is a prevalence of finely carved wood and stone, with nothing more than an elegant ephemera of paper screens between the inhabitants and the world.

The famous tea ceremony was developed by fifteenth-century Buddhist priests as a way of keeping alert during lengthy meditation; it still has a quasi-religious air and a bearing on much Japanese interior design.

Within, traditional Japanese houses are fastidiously minimalist. Generally made of wood, at their most basic and rural, they may consist of wooden platforms, covered in matting, which encircle a central open hearth over which hangs a giant black cauldron. Seats are formed naturally by the wooden platforms with typical economy of means. The walls are wood, stained black, and hung with strange straw artefacts of doubtful purpose. Opaque paper is stuck to the fine wooden slats of sliding windows, thereby creating a contemplative and often totally introverted world.

At a more sophisticated level, the same materials are used, but with all the refinement of an art form. There is a geometric harmony in the echoed squares and rectangles of screens, windows and room divisions, all fastidiously constructed from wooden trellis and paper. On entering a Japanese house, the visitor removes his shoes, and the virgin expanse of black-bordered tatami mats attests to extreme cleanliness. No furniture is necessary as the floor serves all purposes, so rooms tend to be small, and not designated to any particular function.

Natural materials – wood, bamboo, paper and matting are used by all with quiet good taste. The respect for the integrity of building materials is carried through to the symbolic plainness of gardens – perfectly manicured compositions of raked gravel, rocks, moss and water. The extraordinary native mastery of strong design and colour is reserved for clothing, the decoration of Buddhist temples and the many festivals or *matsuri*. But even on these grand occasions massed ebullience is very carefully orchestrated in terms of colour and appropriate costume or uniform of the participants.

ZEN KITCHEN
Opposite **A mysterious collection of kitchen equipment of calm sculptural beauty in a Japanese teahouse fastidiously fashioned from natural materials. The light source is a plain paper rectangular box; a mixture of ceramics with strange deep glazes is stacked on a bamboo drainer over which a single tap of polished brass presides. Five bamboo whisks, like teasels, await their call on the wooden wall – tools for unimaginable culinary feats.**

BLIND FAITH
Right **A double layer of sliding paper blinds ensures total privacy and complete ignorance of the world outside. The peaceful, introverted quality of this room is emphasized by the exquisite paucity of its contents; the elegance is intrinsic, a pair of bone-white carved temples and a small cairn of glossy black pebbles are the only decorative additions.**

SLEEPING QUARTERS
Top right **A curtained niche becomes a bedroom space in Bangkok. A shuttered, barred, glassless window invites air into the tropical stillness while a mosquito net protects the sleepers from less welcome elements. The spartan possessions in this room with its tattered silk hangings confer extraordinary calm and dignity.**

DRAGON BRACKET
Bottom right **A vigorous dragon, all mad grins and curlicues, guards the eaves of this cherry-red wooden building in Thailand. Wood is an adaptable material – here it is elaborately panelled, carved, chamfered, routed and made into spindles for a window – traditional woodturning techniques that used to be a familiar part of everyday Western carpentry skills.**

101 WAYS WITH BAMBOO
Far right **Bamboo walls, roof, seats and ladder, in an open loggia in Thailand. The intricately carved door lintel is typical of ornate regional woodwork; the studded wooden boxes are an easily imitated idea.**

From May to October Thailand is a windswept, rainsoaked country. Then for four months after the monsoons the weather is cool and dry, then it becomes hot, and so the seasons revolve. Here are grown rice and rattan, palms, mangroves and tropical hardwoods. There are crocodiles, 12 varieties of poisonous snake, and a gentle people who are mostly Buddhist, whose lives are governed by genteel rituals often concerned with encouraging family unity and ensuring fertility.

The available building materials are thatch and bamboo, and houses – carefully sited to suit the families' ancestors – are built on stilts with a frame of stout bamboo rods. To these are attached woven mats by way of walls and the whole house is covered with a thick and shaggy roof of grass, rattan leaves, or occasionally wooden shingles. Inside there will be sleeping platforms, given a certain degree of privacy by boards or bamboo mats. To escape the ever-present problem of termites and other intrusive creatures, precious food, grain, seeds and tools are stored in a loft at the apex of the roof, reachable only by ladder.

In most Oriental countries, certainly where Buddhism is the prevailing belief, there is a preference for an airy, open wooden architecture, with walls composed of screens that can be rolled up or slid back. The structure is often barn-like with wide overhanging eaves, upswept gable ends, and constructed of bare weathered wood – the inspiration of which may stem from the fact that Buddha found enlightenment in the contemplation of nature while sitting beneath a tree. The traditional house design is supposed to emulate this openness and shelter.

Reverence and respect for nature is also apparent in the layout of houses built around existing natural features such as trees or rocks. In this hot and humid climate there is an obvious practical reason for creating buildings with ephemeral walls and many slatted windows, wide eaves, verandahs and open walkways.

Well-ordered simplicity is the common denominator of much Oriental architecture. Rooms may be small or large, but are unlikely to be cluttered with furniture – most eating, socializing and sleeping take place on the floor. What there is will be low, and probably stack or fold away when not in use giving a feeling of spaciousness to the smallest interior.

ORIENTAL ELEGANCE
Left **Only the murals and the Oriental fretwork above the windows betray the Malay provenance of this courtyard – the shutters and balconies could equally well come from Louisiana or Portugal. Wedgwood colours are a surprising but effective choice for this panelled woodwork with its integral seating.**

BALI TRADITIONAL
Right **Ornately carved, painted and gilded wood adorns a traditional fifteenth-century nobleman's house. The high wooden platform bed is built into the supports for the ribbed and thatched bamboo roof. The bed is guarded from demons by a fierce mythological beast.**

Extra rooms can be added to the simple structure when needed without detracting from the homogeneity of the building, since the same proportions and materials will be used – the basic modular unit is based on multiples of 60cm × 180cm (2ft × 6ft) in Burma, and 90cm × 180cm (3ft × 6ft) (the size of a tatami mat) in Japan.

In bamboo country, the plant serves all sorts of purposes besides being edible and providing the basic building material for making mats and musical instruments, opium pipes, baskets, tea and tobacco boxes, sun and rain hats. It is also hollowed out for small dishes, finely woven for collecting wild honey, and painted with lac as waterproof containers. Winnowing and threshing baskets are woven in elegant herringbone patterns. The handiwork in these objects is very fine, and while life is reduced to utter simplicity, there is nothing ugly – the architecture exploits the natural strength and beauty of bamboo sympathetically, as do all the humble artefacts.

Against this mainly beige background, the women, and to a lesser extent, the men, come arrayed like peacocks – the textiles produced from native hemp and cotton and local dyes are woven on a primitive backstrap loom, to the most simple designs based on permutations of fabric strips, but the end result is rich colour woven in sophisticated variations on basic patterns. Batik and fine cross-stitch embroidery embellish this fine art still further, covering everything from baby clothes to shrouds, and the garments worn for humble potato-picking trips would outshine much of the designer garb to be seen at a film première. Red, natural unbleached cotton and indigo are the most prevalent colours, worn with elaborate collars and bangles of silver and beads and extremely ornate headdresses.

Indonesia has been known as the 'Spice Islands' since the Portuguese discovered it in the sixteenth century, and subsequently the British and the Dutch fought over it. A *soupçon* of the West on an existing exotic mixture of Islam, China and India. Historically, the people of Indonesia made buildings of stone and brick, sometimes glazed terracotta or sandstone, and occasionally decorated with Indian-inspired murals. In Burma there is traditional woodcarving, silverwork and lacquer.

At a more spontaneous level, the people of Indonesia have a taste for dramatic and frightful masks. Like the ceramic devils' heads and dragons on roofs they vanquish evil forces.

BASKET COLLECTION
Above A fine collection of basketwork in Korea bears out the ethnic tradition of making do with what you have – hats, waterproof clothing for monsoon weather, containers of all kinds, cushions, mattresses, curtains, roofs, fences, even rakes can all be made from local bamboo.

NATURAL ARTISTRY
Right In this nineteenth-century South Korean farmhouse, the materials are simple – bowls made from halved pumpkins are about as basic as you can get – but they are beautifully crafted. The finely carved and reeded woodwork pre-empts the work of Charles Rennie Mackintosh by a century or so.

China is a country that straddles different climatic zones – from the desiccated cold spring air of Peking, which is so dry that friction causes electric sparks to shoot; to the warm, moist subtropical climate of the southeast. This is a country where every inch is cultivated, and the conscientious husbandry of the land is obvious.

The concept of yin and yang predisposes the eye to look for contrasts, and in visual terms the most obvious is that between the puritanical sobriety of dress and restrained simplicity of life compared with the extraordinary overload of colour and symbol in temples.

In the northwest of China and in Korea, where there is a huge disparity between summer and winter temperatures, great ingenuity has led to the evolution of a standard type of house, brilliantly adapted to suit climate and available building materials, and known as 'one bright (room), two dark'. Wood is scarce in this region, so the normal building material is pounded earth, erected *in situ*, layer by layer being tamped hard between shuttering boards. Summer rain is countered by pitched tiled roofs, with broad eaves protecting the mud walls.

These simple three-room single-storey buildings always face south, with large windows running across the front facade only. The eaves are angled to allow the maximum amount of low winter sunlight to enter and warm the building, but prevent as much of the torrid summer sun as possible from doing so.

MINIMAL STYLE
Above **The little cupboard could be of Shaker origin but the corrugated iron could not. There is something about this free and easy outdoor collection of slightly battered objects that looks just right in a casual al fresco Australian setting.**

RUGGED MASCULINITY
Right **These Australian architectural elements have a lot in common with Santa Fe style – a wealth of hand-hewn wood and plain rough plaster walls dominated by a big smoke-blackened open fireplace and terracotta tiles on the floor – ideal for hot days and cool nights.**

Australia has a good mixture of peoples and habitats, the common denominator being that out-of-doors is where most of the action takes place. There are Polish, Dutch, German, Chinese, Indonesian, Japanese, Greek, and Indian communities, each bringing a history and nuance of a different world with them. The notion, however, of all Australians living simple lives in the Outback or in *ad hoc* houses in the middle of farmland is erroneous – it is in fact the most urbanized country in the world, with seven out of ten people living in the cities, mainly in mile after mile of unrelieved suburb.

These homes are the realization of a dream – more people in Australia own their own homes than anywhere else in the world. Many of these often unprepossessing box-like houses have their own swimming pool, and the smell of chunks of meat on the 'barbie' fills the air of a summer evening – this is a defiant statement of the precious ideal of *rus in urbe* at a humble level. Some Australians take to travel and turn up all over the globe, but many are content to stay at home and explore small local chauvinistic skirmishes, especially between Sydney and Melbourne, along the lines of the 'Melbourne proves that there is life after death', and 'Sydney lives, Melbourne functions' variety. Sydney, according to the more fortunate of its inhabitants is the 'best address on earth.'

Occasionally there is an outbreak of good taste, but New Money in Australia has often resulted in extremes of style. In the nineteenth century, Walter Scott Gothick was the flavour of the day, and all sorts of municipal buildings have complex brickwork in stripes of red and yellow, crenellations, towers and arched windows. Spanish rococo had its adherents too, and there are fine balconied and pedimented buildings with crisp white swags of plaster fruit adorning richly coloured facades. In the Southern highlands around Sydney there are rusticated Italianate villas standing among the gum trees. Perth has a small ghetto of olde-worlde beamed and diamond-paned mock-tudor houses, dwarfed by giant high-rise *ziggurats*.

The most refined and typically Australian features of urban houses is the delicate elaboration of cast-iron filigree which has a little of New Orleans, a little of old Spain, and in its exuberance, a great deal of Australia about it – eaves,

GREEN MOVEMENT
Top A cool green vine-shaded terrace with the barest of ingredients makes the most seductive invitation.

BARE AND BEAUTIFUL
Bottom A spot of Gauguin, a touch of wicker, and a length of sisal form a sophisticated partnership.

balconies, porticoes, pilasters, are all fronded and frilled, and cast lacy shadows in the strong sunlight. Cast iron fittings were often exported as ballast in the holds of ships.

The Strand arcade in Sydney – an extravagance of curlicued ironwork – is reminiscent of the genteel and airy charms of its twin in Milan, and in more humble towns, Ballarat for example, there are runs of shop fronts elegant with iron balconies and covered arcades left over from their Victorian heyday.

For the rich, there are handsome balconied colonial mansions modelled according to the same formula as Tara in *Gone with the Wind*, with Palladian proportions, broad verandahs and cloisters. The clapboard frontages and dusty boardwalks of many of the restored Gold-Rush towns are familiar from their American counterparts in any Western. There are strongly painted brick shop fronts in provincial towns like Geelong which could have come from *Early Sunday Morning* by Edward Hopper, so bold is their colour, so classic their architecture and harshly sunlit their facades. At the most humble end of the architectural scale, there is a strong Edwardian and British influence in the strings of paintbox bright clapboard beachhouses that festoon the shore of Port Phillip Bay.

In the country, building is often a matter of ingenuity and expediency. In the unrelieved heat of opal mining country people dig underground homes, with all the usual *mod cons* to keep cool. Wooden shacks still serve to house gold-prospectors, and there is a certain impoverished dignity in these temporary dwellings of silvered timber lathes. The same elements, sometimes with a more solid and protective overcoat of plaster, make up the Outback vernacular. The timber may be refined and turned or carved to make bargeboards mimicking iron lace, the roof is quite likely to make use of corrugated iron – there is a casual pragmatism about turning very basic raw materials, barely modified, into a house. Rooms may be added on a whim to the existing structure, and floored or not – bare earth will do if nothing better turns up. Sheets of corrugated plastic, when used to construct roofs, may cast a strange aqueous light indoors, large overhanging eaves provide a breezy and shaded outdoor space in which to work or just laze in this benign climate.

SUNSHINE AND SHADE
Top left **Unusual Chinoiserie in a little family of bamboo furniture has an airiness appropriate to this wisteria-fringed sitting area.**

COBBLED LOGGIA
Bottom left **An ambiguous no man's land between indoors and out, with a mixture of objects usually confined to one or the other. The washstand, spotlit by a beam of sunlight, is a natural home for every kind of footwear, while a composition of hats, saddles and a bicycle completes a sportive picture.**

RUNIC WALLPAINTING
Right **Possibly an altar to the divine sausage, this strongly (and strangely) original mural gives a definite personality to an otherwise unremarkable hallway.**

THE AMERICAS

Huge and unmanageably various, America is a melting pot of cultures, with strands and threads of many nationalities running through the population. The two triangular continents of North and South America stretch from Alaska, almost touching Russia at the Bering Strait in the North, to Cape Horn in the South, and encompass terrain as diverse as ice flows and tropical swamps. Contemporaneous with the glittering architectural stalagmites that characterize the New York skyline, chunks of the past remain – there are still many Navajo and Cherokee speakers, and a remaining disciple or two of Mother Ann Lee, the first Shaker, hangs on to a celebrated celibacy in the Shaker villages of Sabbathday Lake (Maine) and Canterbury (New Hampshire). With hands dedicated to work, hearts to God, the Shakers remain firmly espoused to the virtues of plainness.

SIMPLE HEARTH
A basic and pleasing Santa Fe-style adobe fireplace is flanked by a pair of macho paling and leather chairs.

LONG ISLAND LOG CABIN
Above **The barest essentials in a naive do-it-yourself home, whose Long Island location is at variance with its country-style ruggedness: heating comes by log, lighting by paraffin. A patchwork poppy on the bed puns with the flower basket.**

TIN PICKINGS
Right **Ebullient flowers and berries adorn Pennsylvanian tinware, their rich dark colours palely echoed in the painted wooden shelf. Old tins can easily be found in antique shops and markets and transformed by repainting with traditional motifs.**

BASIC BATH-HOUSE
Opposite **This simple yet sophisticated Long Island bathroom suggests a self-conscious Zen retreat from the complicated rigours of New York executive life. A mixture of folk style and bucolic country whimsy contribute to the decoration of this house.**

North America has a strong backbone made up from a Protestant work ethic, prevailing virtues of true grit, toughness, persistence and simplicity. A combination of native Indian courage and frontier values that is enhanced by an admixture of patient endurance, contributed by the legions of emigrants who have found a home there.

Those settlers who followed Columbus found quite a repertoire of indigenous decorative expertise with which to augment the ideas they brought from Europe. And where the native inhabitants, in this case the North American Indians, strike upon a good and economic notion, the sensible settler is reluctant to waste it. So in the far north where red-haired Russians have descendants among the Athapaskan Indians close to the Bering Strait, solid log cabins remain. Organic structures by the Yukon river in a landscape of birch, spruce, willow and aspen, are low and almost windowless to cope with heavy snow and a regular temperature dip to minus 20°C (0°F), the unchanged descendants of North West Coast Indian log houses.

Log and plywood cabins are at the butch end of the wooden architecture spectrum. More rarefied building styles – the colonial clapboard house for example – evolved with this classic North American building material, whose regular symmetrical style and fine details always look good. In fact, even the most absurdly anachronistic and pretentious of Greek temple porticoes has charm because of the casual fluency with which this vernacular architecture is achieved. New Jersey, the Berkshires, New England, Norfolk, Virginia, and Annapolis, Maryland, have an old-world sophistication of desirable clapboard houses in sand, earth and sky colours, crisply delineated with white doorframes and architraves.

Scattered just about everywhere in the United States are reminders of other times and other cultures. Pockets of hardy Norwegian and Russian immigrants survive the icy chill of a North Dakota winter in distinctly Scandinavian rust-red clapboard farmhouses, whose tiny windows are firmly shut against the whipping snow. In Pennsylvania there are the pristine homes and neat farms of the Amish and the Friesland Mennonites, and interesting traditions from German, Irish, Polish, Italian, Mexican, Bulgarian, Lithuanian and Vietnamese immigrants.

Mother Ann Lee, the founder of the Shaker movement, came from Manchester, England. One of eight children, she was born in 1736 and belonged to a beleaguered sect known as the Shaking Quakers. The Shakers believed that the second coming of Christ was imminent and they prepared themselves for this by withdrawing from the outside world into their own communities and dedicating their hearts to God and their hands to work. This communal life also insisted on equality of the sexes and common ownership of possessions. Mother Lee sailed to America in 1774 and settled at Niskayuna, eight miles north-west of Albany, New York where she formed the first Shaker community. The influential relics of Shaker life, those quietly elegant chairs and tables, oval boxes and simple architecture, all embodying symmetry, order and function – 'religion in wood' – are concentrated mostly in Massachusetts and neighbouring states. The philosophy behind their much-emulated artefacts came from Mother Ann: 'Do all your work as though you had a thousand years to live, and as you would if you knew you must die tomorrow'. Shaker style has not been universally admired, however – Nathaniel Hawthorne was repelled: 'Everything so neat that it was a pain and a constraint to look at it'.

Unlike the Amish, the Shakers were always interested in technology, and had a fine streak of inventiveness – they developed the washing machine, flat broom, efficient wood-burning stoves, and water-resistant fabric. They are credited with being the first to packet seeds in a neat and transportable way. They were often the first to install electricity and telephones. And nothing was too humble – the charm of a Shaker interior is partly its homogeneity. Every single thing from bobbins to barns is simply, logically and beautifully made, a unity of purpose and belief being displayed in the objects they made. Characteristic objects produced by Shaker craftsmen are spindle-back rocking chairs, trundle beds and, probably most distinctive of all, Shaker boxes. These were made in their thousands and sold either singly or in matching sets, in graduated nests that could be used for storing tools, sewing equipment or groceries. One of the sect wrote: 'A man can show his religion as much in measureing (sic) onions as... in singing glory halalua...'

SHAKER SIMPLICITY
Top right **Shaker artefacts are the perfect combination of beauty and utility. The corner of a bedroom at Mount Vernon Shaker Community shows such spartan minimalism that even the addition of an apple begins to look like a touch of frivolity. The tongued-and-grooved door is painted in traditional casein-based paint.**

THE BARE ESSENTIALS
Bottom right **Pigeon-grey paint with the bloom of purple grapes, finishes window and skirting in Shaker style. In this supreme expression of 'less is more', every object has more than its fair share of importance, allowing the subtle colours to become major decorative components.**

PLAIN TRUTH
Far right **Wood, pewter and cane are honest, unadorned materials, beautified only with the rich patina conferred by time and care. In this kitchen of the Porter-Phelps Huntington House in Massachusetts, doors, dado and shutters are painted with the same grey-green paint.**

HANDMADE IN SANTA FE
Above **A simple building, whose raw materials are the earth and wood by which it stands; its flat roof is supported by logs, and its adobe walls are finished with sinuous hand-smoothed curves.**

TRADITIONAL MATERIALS
Right **Only the electric light fitting in this Santa Fe interior hints at twentieth-century sophistication – the rest could have been put together centuries ago, and has a smooth and sculptural simplicity directly descended from ancient methods.**

The indigenous Native American Indians did not all lead nomadic lives following the buffalo, then rustling up a teepee or a wigwam whenever they needed to sleep. North-West-coast Indians built sophisticated single-storey plank and beam houses, inhabited by several families – theirs are the dugouts, masks, and handsome totem poles that we consider 'standard' Indian, while the Navajo and Hopi Indians of Arizona and New Mexico adopted a style of architecture using mud and clay with similarities to the Spanish and North African adobe style. The Lakes Indians' wigwams, Sioux summer lodges and Iroquois long houses were more ephemeral structures made of poles covered with sheets of bark, and the hunting tribes of the plains made teepees out of 15–50 buffalo cow hides sewn with sinew and beautifully decorated with paint – now unfortunately just a playground legacy, if that.

Like anything that has suddenly been spotted to have commercial potential, North American Indian art and artefacts today are very uneven in quality, but bowls, baskets, textiles and bead-work created as souvenirs, often have more than a ghost of their historic fastidious and spirited craftsmanship. In the past, baskets were twined from split willow, hazel and redbud, coiled baskets as big as a small car were made from grass and rushes, plaited baskets from the separated layers of oak, ash and hickory; spruce, cedar bark and fern root were used for especially fine artistry. Indian pottery, usually in rich earth colours, is still made in prehistoric forms and painted with geometric shapes or stylized birds and animals.

Textiles remain one of the most attractive Indian arts – they once used buffalo, goat, moose and specially-bred dog hair, as well as fibres from cotton, hemp, nettle, milkweed and cedar and basswood bark. Navajo women and Hopi men still use the simple belt loom constructed from sticks introduced from Mexico in the 1st century AD, with which to make brightly coloured sashes. Large vertical blanket looms may have been invented in the southwest, and upon them the Hopi make subtle blue, cream or black woollen Pueblo blankets, and Navajo weavers continue to make the brilliant striped rugs regarded by many as traditionally Indian. In fact, they evolved only after exposure to imported techniques and materials in the 1860s.

TILE PATCHWORK
Left **Rough grace in a covered entrance courtyard. Floored with chunks of stone upon which spouts an incongruous fountain, a piece of cooling kitsch that is forgivable in a hot climate. There is an absent-minded charm about the bright agglomeration of tiles, and a casual breeziness in the wrought iron gate and window.**

BRILLIANT SHUTTERS
Left A collection of shuttered entrances in Haiti, where subtle colours simply disappear in bright sun. There is an unselfconscious freedom with paint, unconstrained by perfectionist principles – slatted doors, panels, hinges and dados are roughly picked out in colours of startling contrast. Casual abandonment of fussy niceties matters not at all. The tall, narrow doors, with their slatted ventilation panels and skylight slits, are typical of the Creole culture.

The West Indies, Dominica, Haiti and Cuba are true islands in the sun, where the fidgeting rigour of the work ethic is replaced by a relaxed notion that *being* might be more important than *doing*. Nothing is ever quite finished, because there are always better ways of spending time than filling and sanding. And in place of the restrained good taste of Colonial and Williamsburg greys, ochres, and dusty greens, there is unleashed a startling rainbow of pure, bright shameless colour and pattern with folkloric significance; a decorative pyramid painted on a wall harking back to folk-memories of Egypt; a particular soft bright blue guaranteed to ward off any lurking evil spirits.

Rain and cold are not enemies here, a do-it-yourself movable chattel house constructed from a single skin of wooden planks suffices, providing the sun shines and the walls inside and out are a joyous sugar pink and turquoise, or sky blue and buttercup. All you need is a small verandah from which to enjoy the carefully rehearsed swagger of the local talent. Where the weather is your friend and the sun is almost harsh in its brightness, there can be great pleasure in such pure subsistence.

Wood, wattle, corrugated iron, thatch and paint – these are the simple raw materials for an easy, relaxed architecture. Beyond this there is an exuberant eclecticism in the elements – though the basic structure is as strictly geometric as a child's drawing, the details have a cheeky international air and may include Greek pilasters, Roman porticoes, African thatchery and Hispanic ceramics, all bound together with a frill of fretwork bargeboard introduced from the United States.

In Cuba there is a strong flavour of southern Spain, from the baroque facade of Havana cathedral: 'Music turned to stone' in the words of the novelist Alejo Carpentier, to the wooden balconies, tiled roofs and turrets recalling Moorish Granada in the back streets. Echoes of nineteenth century wealth and sophistication remain in dilapidated neoclassical houses with delicate stained-glass fanlights over shuttered French doors and windows. In Haiti, poverty and corrugated iron prevail, but even temporary shacks are painted in glowing shrimp pink and aquamarine, lampposts and litter bins are striped with scarlet and emerald paint.

MEXICAN CLOISTER
Above The rough textures of the spiky agaves on the roofline merge with surprising colours in a lantern-lit atrium. Peach, plum and fuchsia commit luminous warfare on walls and mouldings, while the dazzling colour scheme is finished off with a tasteful mural.

QUIRKY BRILLIANCE
Opposite Frida Kahlo's house is a unique hybrid between childishness and genius. She had a restless and iconoclastic talent.

STRANGE FRUIT
Top far right An irreverent still life with fruit in Kahlo's house – even the kitchen table is a source of ideas. Anyone could paint birds and flowers on a yellow ground and enjoy their battered charm.

FREEDOM CERAMICS
Bottom far right A good extrovert mixture of tiles in a Mexican kitchen – the loose haphazard design is a positive element here, since a careful finish and punctilious matching would kill this brilliant kaleidoscope.

In common with many parts of the planet where dry and dusty earth is the chief building material, the defiant, cheerful spirit of Mexican decoration is most often expressed in paint. Houses, streets, ceramics and tiles deny their common denominator of dust in a pyrotechnic display of colour – always the decorative wealth of the poor. The most humble shack can outdo a palace by the sheer inventiveness of bold, simple colour applied to its walls, inside and out. Sherbet yellow, for instance, in vivid, electric partnership with cobalt blue produces a unique and fiercely Mexican style. There is no fear of impact here, no inhibitions dictated by the embarrassed confines of 'good taste'. White and terracotta are the base colours to which are added a paintbox of multicoloured tiles, polychrome statuary, walls washed in magenta, orange and violet, and climbing flame-flowered bougainvillea. Architectural details are picked out with borders of paint, tiles, and the celebrated Mexican art of fresco panels. These insouciant decorative additions add richness and interest to a building that might otherwise seem quite plain and draw attention to its architectural features.

Typically the Mexican house revolves around a courtyard which is floored with tiles or pebbles and furnished with a chair or two, a hammock slung like a rainbow in reverse between two pillars, and a few massive and rotund flower pots spilling blossom on to the scene. Within, shady rooms are sparsely furnished, but filled with touches of brightness – a shocking pink rug arguing with terracotta floor tiles, a scarlet tablecloth or an acid yellow niche in a thick wall acting as a counterpoint to an otherwise clean, white interior. Glittering objects of punched and painted tin, and widely striped curtains separating one room from another, all provide punctuation points within an interior.

Spanish influence is most evident in heavy, carved and panelled wooden furniture. Curvaceous armoires and dressers of matronly proportions prevail, their pompous solidity subverted by the irreverent cheek of decorative details startled into life with yellow, viridian and purple. This restless celebration of colour and kitsch is reminiscent of the decorative style enjoyed in Rajasthan – it is the creative defiance of the human spirit when presented with a dusty, monochrome natural world.

Central and South America are the homes of organic and masterly earth architecture: curvaceous bone-white adobe houses akin to African mud dwellings but with an almost sedate influence from Spanish and Portuguese culture, most visible in ecclesiastical artefacts, tiles and marvellous, ornately carved heavy wooden coffers and doors. Pre-Spanish and Peruvian buildings still exist whose internal structure, supported by pillars made from tree trunks, creates a smooth sculptural sinuosity of white painted mud that is like the sun-bleached rib cage of a fossilized dinosaur.

Simple and spartan building materials contrast vibrantly with intricate decorative details and an undiluted kaleidoscope of colours used for ceramics and clothing. Peruvian and Guatemalan textiles are knitted, embroidered or woven from cotton or the wool of the native alpaca or llama and dyed to startling brightness, achieving raw rainbows of colour. Themes and motifs from the ancient art of Peru such as the feline, bird, serpent and human figure still prevail in both ceramics and textiles. Many of these date from around 300AD when the religion placed great emphasis on the cult of the dead, and funeral offerings to prominent citizens became very ornate. Hammocks are knotted in fine filigree cotton and mythical events are appliquéd in throbbing primary colours to Panamanian *molas*. In Brazil, houses of wooden slats with floors of beaten earth are adorned with runic tapestries, scarlet painted cupboards and anachronistic still-lifes of glittering stainless steel cooking pans.

NAIVE COLLECTION
Far left Idiosyncratic containers and a vigorous painting from St. Kitts are bound together visually by the strong common denominator of tan and canary colours. The terracotta picks up the red and brown hues from the painting and the ultimate effect is one of vitality and warmth.

SPARTAN ELEGANCE
Left Geometric encaustic tiles here form a cool shining floor; seating ranges from an uncomfortable interpretation of a *bergère* sofa to a carved throne. When the impressive shutters are closed, the whole bare interior is lit by a distantly twinkling 40-watt light bulb.

TACTILE VARIETY
Below top A shady verandah, filled with sculptural objects and contrasts of rough and smooth textures.

RIVER BEDS
Bottom As close to nature as one could be, these bunks are in a tree-house eyrie which offers an unequalled view of river and jungle.

CREATING THE LOOK

The point about much ethnic decoration is that it is simple. Basic materials and tools preponderate, and much of the best is an exercise in the magic properties of the imagination. Anyone can achieve an ethnic look; anyone can take inspiration from the wedding-cake intricacies of Russian wooden window-frames and adapt them to make a flat-painted – or even three-dimensional *trompe l'oeil* for the more ambitious – indoor equivalent to surround window or doorway; anyone can analyse and emulate the family of colours in a vivid Mexican kitchen, or copy the integrity of the natural materials in a Japanese interior. This book is a guide to an exciting repertoire of different attitudes and styles, some urbane, some bucolic, spontaneous or deliberate, traditional or there are those as new and varied as a magpie's hoard.

It does not take very much – ethnic is a look based on the simplest of objects and materials. A length of fabric – unevenly printed indigo and white, sunset-striped textiles from Ghana, familiar Indian woodblock-printed paisley cotton – can lend an exotic and foreign air to beds or windows, and transform low seating with Northern African opulence, requiring only fretwork grilles, geometric tiles and a hookah to complete the look.

Authenticity is all very well, but harmony of decoration and colour are more satisfying to the humble amateur

of interior design – you want to create an atmosphere that gives you pleasure, not research a dissertation. Therefore, do not hesitate to partner the wood of one continent with the textiles of another – if your kelim from Northern Africa has the right kind of colours to go with a carved wooden box from Spain and a pair of painted Kashmiri candlesticks, alive with a miniaturist's repertoire of tiny birds and flowers, then put them all together and enjoy the chemistry. There are no rules to be broken, except an intuition for what looks good. You may decide that the ensemble needs a saffron-coloured wall to bring out the underlying common denominator of colour – paint is the easiest and quickest way of unifying a disparate composition. Pastiche is not to be despised – the illustrations in this book are an inspiring source of ideas, and you will find faking and forging unexpected paint techniques and designs is profoundly satisfying.

Elements from one material transpose into another – you may not have the desire or equipment to knock off a pile of peasant plates, but the colours and design might well make the perfect border for a painted box, or you might daringly try your hand at papier mâché and steal the shape with which to experiment. There is comfort and inspiration in the fact that somewhere people have made these things and live with them – you may not have thought about painting your house with muted earth-coloured zig-zags, but you might take courage and experiment with variations on the idea in a small and unimportant room, knowing too that where the zig-zags came from, they were not intended to last for ever. Look for the soul and the spirit in decorative objects.

Then there is the joy of recycling. In Mexico and North Africa the humble tin is cut and shaped and punched and painted and ends up being a mask, a constellation of Christmas decorations, a candlestick or a twinkling lampshade. And the thrifty transmutation of a pile of old clothes into plaited or prodded rag rugs, or the intricate complexities of patchwork in the Amish tradition, is a cheering insult to the trashy planned obsolescence which is all around us and rarely questioned. And of course there is the straightforward pleasure of going into an antique shop, or rootling at a market stall, and making an inspired and informed choice – picking up the right indigo and white burnished Cameroon cloth to pull your heterogeneous collection of African wood and brass together. Your crucial acquisition may cost nothing – black lacquer and matting may already exist in your life, just awaiting a still life of smooth, rounded pebbles and a sea-silvered branch picked up from a local beach to become a shrine that you need not be a Buddhist to respect.

Wood

Wherever trees grow, wood is often the most obvious building material for houses, whether exteriors – steps, door and window frames, shutters, balconies, verandahs and roofs; or interiors – seats, boxes, tables, screens and bowls. Wood lends itself to all sorts of domestic paraphernalia from the smallest and most beautifully finished oval Shaker box, to the roughest, most robust Finnish sauna. There are few homes where wood is not present in some form or other because it is so infinitely adaptable. Apart from the sheer variety of different woods it is one of the most durable materials.

The pine forests of the northern hemisphere immediately spring to mind as the birthplace of variations on a timber theme, whether an American log cabin or a colonial clapboard dwelling; a Russian *dacha* or the complex mortice-and-tenon constructions of China and Japan.

HOMAGE TO WOOD
A Scandinavian interior where timber, rough-hewn or turned and carved, is almost the total picture.

In America, white pine (*Pinus strobus* and *Pinus monticola*) is used in painted, panelled interiors, where its smooth, easily worked grain can be exploited to full advantage. For an authentic matt finish, use durable casein paint or ordinary emulsion finished off with a coat of beeswax – this sort of timber does need protection.

Longleaf pine (*Pinus palustris*) is often used as an exterior wood. It has a close-grained and long-lasting resinous heartwood, which matures and polishes well. The Scots pine (*Pinus sylvestris*) is commonly found in Europe, from Scandinavia to northern Spain, and from the North Sea to Kamchatka in Russia. It provides the yellow deal from which most pine furniture is made. Scots pine heartwood is a deep red-brown colour, formed by its resin which acts as a preservative, producing a timber that can be as durable as oak, depending on where and how quickly it was grown.

Interior walls of North American log cabins and Scandinavian houses often show the rough unevenness imparted by their primitive pit-sawn or riven finish, or they may still bear the marks of the adze or plane. Wax polish or Danish oil and the patina of age, use and wood-smoke is a sympathetic treatment, but polyurethane varnish is not. Scandinavian interiors are often painted, while Shaker and Japanese interiors tend towards perfectionist understatement, with all the beauty of the natural grain and colour exploited to the full.

The wood used in Japanese interiors is often stained a dark rich brown, which shows up the moiré finish of the grain, and can be partnered by a collection of screens, black-handled drawers, and sliding doors in different woods and natural materials. Screens can be created from strips of wood or square-section solid trellis, carefully framed and detailed around heavy tissue paper which is given a slight sheen and transparency by being coated with linseed oil. The rich shiny black (or red) of Japanese lacquer can be achieved with a couple of coats of enamel on a perfectly smooth base which has been gessoed, if necessary, and then coated with six or more layers of oil-tinted varnish and rubbed down meticulously with 600-grit wet and dry paper in between each application. Finish the final coat by rubbing down with pumice, rottenstone and oil to obtain a perfectionist gloss.

JAPANESE SOPHISTICATION
Top left Every tiny detail of this exquisitely made Japanese interior is the final expression of centuries of thoughtful evolution. The materials – wood, paper and ceramics – are all natural and simple enough, but their finished, calm perfection has little to do with nature.

SHAKER SPARTAN
Bottom left The well-ordered essentials of life again, but with a more human feel – the wood is slightly worn and has retained more of its natural character producing a rarefied blend of art and craft.

FINNISH RUSTIC
Opposite Hearty and rugged lumberjack architecture, whose wooden imperfections are openly relished, tones well with a handwoven hanging and a bright patchwork quilt.

NAIVE AMERICAN
Above left **There is a self-conscious naivety about this interior that is somewhat subverted by the unfortunate addition of an aluminium ceiling light. However, the broad bands of horizontal timber offer a strong and simple finish, and the yellow colour applied to them is both original and practical , successfully lightening an otherwise very wooden and dark, almost moody, antiquescape.**

REFINED ISLAMIC
Above right **A North African doorway has a triple embellishment of carving, painting and tiling, all quietly and subtly controlled by a pinkish-brown common denominator.**

MONUMENTAL RUSSIAN
Above left **Huge chunks of untreated wood have been roughly dovetailed together to make an arch, then chamfered and routed into sunburst panels on a sturdy door. The end result is deceptively simple in appearance, belying the generous use of materials. The nails have rusted and the wood has weathered to form a punctuated moiré design.**

BRIGHT HAITI
Above right **The wood here, however nicely cut and fitted, is an excuse for a rainbow application of gloss paint, the moulding a vehicle for a startling interplay of bright primary colours.**

PAINTED PANELS
Above **A Greek bedroom whose wall of cupboard fronts is brightly painted in red, green and yellow. A folksy colour scheme carried out with perfectionist élan. Nearly matching, but not quite, are the woven rugs.**

RICH AND REFINED
Opposite **A stunning room on the island of Patmos, where walls, doors, niches and ingenious built-in furniture have all been brocaded with paint and 'embroidered' with colour. The repeating stripes of pattern on a warm ochre background transmute to richer, darker colours along the wall in a confection of luscious excess.**

Touches of gilding on mouldings can be achieved very simply by burnishing gilt paste wax on a black, cinnabar or dark wood background. Crackle glaze has a look of Oriental sophistication and can be mimicked without great difficulty. Use two layers of incompatible paint which dry at different rates – for example, a dry base colour painted over with a clear varnish. Wait until a skin has formed but the varnish is not quite dry, and apply a layer of emulsion. More colour can be wiped into the emulsion if it seems necessary, then when it is absolutely dry, seal with a couple of coats of varnish.

The ancient, silvered look of heavy Spanish and South American woodwork can be emulated if doors are made from an open-grained wood such as oak. Wire brush the door in the direction of the grain to open the pores. Either use a paste of 4.4kg (2lb) lump lime to 3.4l (6 pints) of water; a 50/50 thinned white oil-based paint, or ready-made liming wax. Work it well into the grain, smooth off the surface and remove the surplus before it dries. Buff the wood and then seal with transparent polish or clear varnish.

Panelled and tongued-and-grooved timber invite decoration. Stencils are the easiest method of decorating wood. Use strong and subtle non-chemical (natural pigment) colours, and finish off with hand-painted touches and hints of gilding. Begin by colourwashing the bare wood thinly with raw umber. When it is dry, use a wide paintbrush to apply a layer of emulsion, thinned with water to the consistency of milk. Paint it on evenly, in the direction of the grain and allow to dry overnight. If the colour is rich enough you can apply your design straightaway, but you may be tempted to repeat the previous process with another similar, darker or contrasting coat of thinned emulsion. When the background colour looks right, stencil the panels or strips of timber using emulsion and a stencil cut out with a surgical blade from thick transparent acetate or stencil card on a cutting mat. Do not apply the colour too thickly as there should be variety in the tone and shading towards the edge of the motif – a small sponge gives a good open texture. Extra details can be added freehand if desired. When the paint is dry, if it still looks too solid, try sanding it gently to break up any hard edges, and then finish with a couple of coats of lightly-tinted umber varnish.

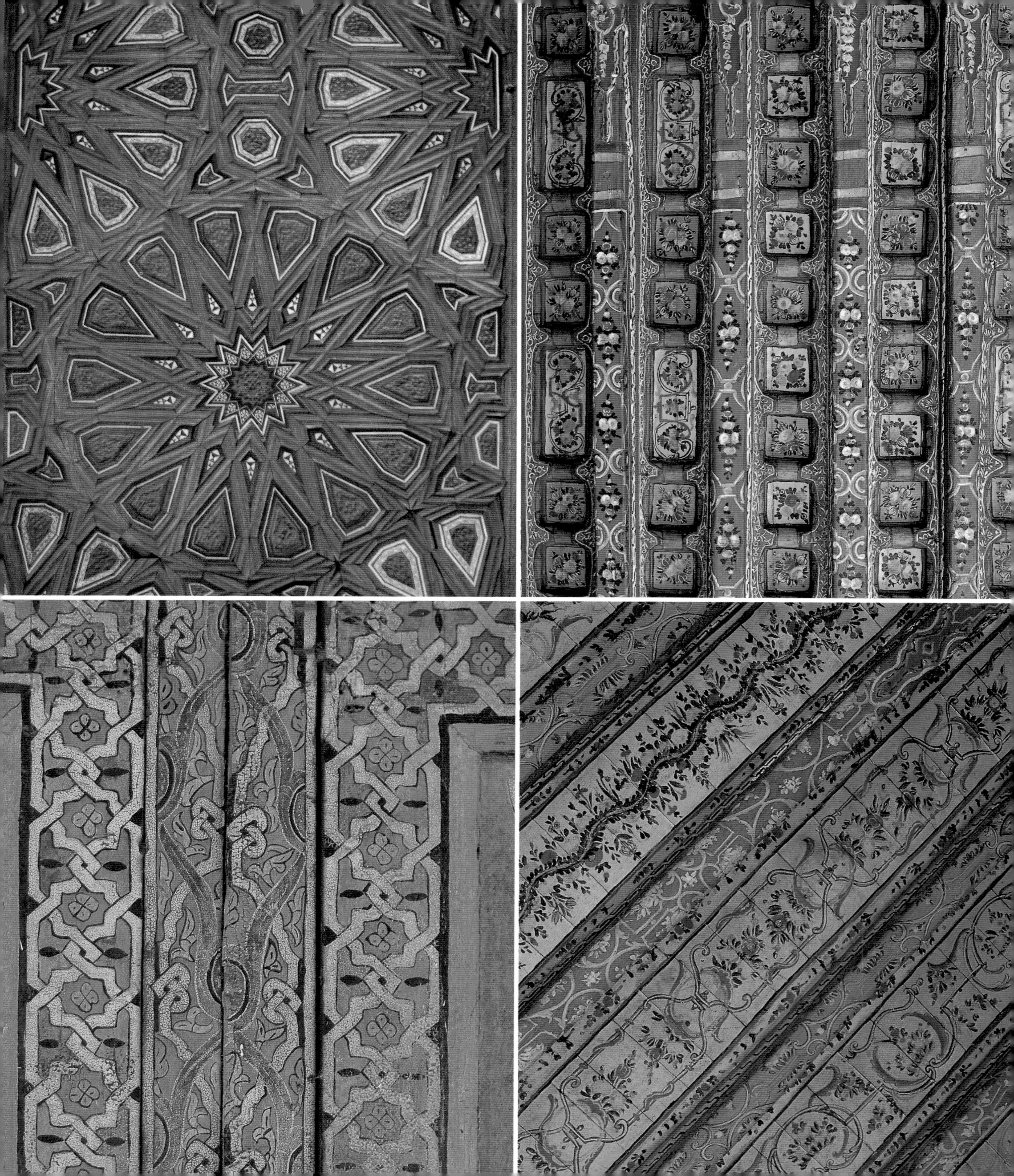

ART OF WOOD
Opposite top left **A ceiling vaulted with an Islamic star design, carved and painted in wood.**
Opposite top right **Coffering on a ceiling is elaborately painted with a flurry of tiny roses.**
Opposite bottom left and right **Detail from a pair of doors, whose intricate painted finish has been cracked and faded by weather to create a subtle mixture of old-fashioned colours.**

PURDAH VIEW
Top right **A balcony in North Africa built with the original intention of keeping women hidden, while allowing them a tantalizing glimpse of the man's world outside.**
Bottom right **The filigree outlook from a Moroccan household, screened from the world behind elaborately carved panels of wood.**

To give wood a matt, worn look in a single colour, casein paints can be rubbed back to give them an air of antiquity. They do not form a skin, but will come off in a powdery fashion, exposing a convincingly-worn patch of bare timber. For intricate, many-coloured carvings, water-based paints such as acrylic or even emulsion are the easiest to use as they dry quickly and are the most controllable. Sand back the area where you want to create a worn surface, rub in a spot of fuller's earth to fake the dust of ages, a touch of gilding paste to add richness, and polish vigorously twice with beeswax to seal and protect the final result. Remember that most carved and painted wood is all the better for casual imperfections.

Occasionally a very fine hand-painted pattern is needed – maybe you want to paint your coffered ceiling; or you may bravely decide to give your kitchen cupboards a Moorish look; start by sanding down your chosen object (bare wood is best, so existing paint must be very thoroughly sanded) and giving it a couple of coats of emulsion (thinned down with water or stippled on with a brush or sponge for an interesting, lively texture). Designs can be taken from anywhere, but to save yourself nervous exhaustion, it is best if they are in the same proportions as the object of your labour. You may alter the size of the design you are using by drawing it out freehand onto tracing paper with a soft pencil, then using graph paper beneath to work out geometric patterns.

Attach the tracing paper, pencil side down, to the prepared object and trace the design onto the base coat with a hard pencil. Reverse the paper to trace the other half if the design is symmetrical. Exact precision is not as important as a lively line. If your design or border is fairly simple and repetitive you could make a guide such as the undulating templates used by Welsh quilters to ensure regular structure and spacing, and then fill in small details by eye. For one-off designs, such as strutting cockerels and chickens, a few discreet freehand pencil strokes as a guide to the placement and proportions should suffice, and a practice run on a piece of card will enable you to perfect your fluid line. Paint on your design with a good sable artist's brush and acrylic paint, thinned with water to the consistency of single cream.

Acrylic paint dries fast on wood, so it is easy to use and means that you can carry on painting without a break. When you have finished, take a critical look at your handiwork after a short absence – it might need a little more background texture, which you can supply by dabbing on dots of colour using a chopstick or a cotton bud, or small clouds of gold using gilding paste and a make-up sponge. You can outline or accentuate the geometry of the design with gold lines. Break the sharp outlines, and wear down appropriate corners and handled areas with fine glasspaper. Let it dry overnight, and then brush on a thin coat of wax-based varnish.

If your heart's desire is to have a guardian angel at the head of your bed or to decorate the panels of an armoire with botanical prints (see opposite), the humble art of découpage or even repeating hand-coloured photocopies is not to be despised. Seal the cutout picture or photocopy using PVA adhesive diluted with an equal amount of water. Colour your photocopy with acrylic, gouache or watercolour paint and let it dry. You may want to start off by giving it a background wash of colour to blend with the ultimate background and break the startling whiteness of the paper. When it is perfectly dry and you are happy with it, seal with PVA adhesive or varnish and when that has dried, attach your artwork motif to the piece of furniture with wallpaper glue or more PVA. A *trompe l'oeil* rustic frame can be painted over the edges with acrylic if you wish, or a rosebud border applied around your botanical print. Proprietary crackle varnish or nicotine-brown French enamel varnish will give your handiwork an Old Testament antiquity.

Much can be done with borders and frames – simple geometric patterns or small, easy repeating floral designs accentuating details of carpentry, panels and mouldings have more impact than the ease of doing them would suggest. Almost all applied paintwork looks better for a little ageing, and it does not matter whether it is achieved by sanding or by applying an overlay of tinted or crackle varnish.

It takes real confidence to succeed with bright, naive freehand designs, and the situation must be right. Somehow, strong sunshine is a prerequisite to make primary colours behave – but if you've got it, enjoy it. Protect your finished work with a clear lacquer or varnish.

FURNISH WITH PAINT
Opposite top left **A spring-like hen and cockerel on a solid little cupboard door are painted in fresh, bright colours combined with lots of white.**
Opposite centre left **A finely painted and endearingly tatty Finnish armoire. Its panels are picked out and edged in solid primary colours, and embellished with flowers. The centre front fillet of roses is a particularly pretty detail, and cheeringly easy to copy.**
Opposite bottom left **A worn cupboard front in soft Scandinavian colours. The subtle matt finish could be emulated by applying water-based paint and beeswax.**
Opposite **A daunting encouragement to think worthy thoughts on settling to sleep. The fine paintwork is apparently Scandinavian, though the flavour is Italian.**
Above **A Mexican heterogeneity of painted objects designed to give heart to anyone who has left a prize possession half-painted. The roughly applied colour has great charm.**

If you have a piece of furniture with a strong decorative line, carved and curlicued and crying out to be noticed, it might be a suitable case for paint treatment – chalky bright colours to pick out the unusual details are right in a Mediterranean climate and several paint companies include these colours in their range. Beneath muddier skies subtle effects such as verdigris, rust or gilding might be less of a shock.

Wooden fretwork panels are a North African and Indian speciality, as a more durable alternative to lace curtains for a private view. They respond well to liming and can be used as delicate interior walls or screens, round a galleried bedroom for example, and cast a wonderfully filigreed light on the space within.

Collections and displays need objective thought. Brightly-coloured shelving becomes a decorative item in itself and dominates whatever sits upon it. For an eclectic display, it is a good idea to pin down a common denominator of colour, and run it as a theme, although there is something almost sinister in slavish obsessions with particular types of china – blue and white

SOUTH AMERICAN PASTICHE
Opposite top left **It takes very few elements to create an ethnic look – humble shelves painted bright yellow are a good start. Combine them with a painted and battered carved chair, a brilliant Guatemalan throw, and a sprinkling of peasant pots to complete the look.**

NORTH AMERICAN NAIVE
Left **A lighthearted conglomeration of folk art pieces creates a sophisticated display. The objects are wittily balanced on vases, glasses and plastic containers to give height. This is the eclectic residue of enlightened travel, rather than the result of hours of labour put in by the owner to create hand-whittled artefacts.**

A MEXICAN PAST
Right **A fine shrine to strange gods, beautifully shown off in a custom-built shelving unit. The predominant stone colours glow warmly against a cornflower-blue background.**

for example. Groups of toning colour look best together, and trying out combinations of objects on different coloured backgrounds will sometimes reveal the perfect counterpoint or common denominator. Occasionally an appropriate setting can give cohesion to a collection of objects; a lacquer cabinet, for example, could provide a flattering home for carved Chinese *chops* (printing stamps). A strongly developed theme, spiked with a few variations to add piquancy, is the look to aim for.

You are creating a still life, and with collections, presentation is all – if you do happen to possess the comprehensive and complete works of an obscure and revered Etruscan potter, the least you can do is to cast a quizzical eye in their direction with a view to pairing them with the most flattering background, and displaying them to show off all their finer points. It is not necessary to have an elaborate display cabinet either. In fact, stairwells make rather good viewing places, since you get a changing prospect on a display, and a modular custom-built unit is relatively simple to make.

RATTAN

HOUSE OF STRAW
A flimsy structure in India is fashioned from panelled basketwork and painted a glowing aquamarine. The owner seems perfectly satisfied with the end result.

Rattan cane, wicker, bamboo, rush, palm leaves – these are the *sine qua non* of the tropics, and fulfil a million functions. The Chinese describe rattan and wicker as 'Supple and strong, like the Chinese character'. It is this which makes these materials a practical choice for a huge variety of purposes, from sophisticated verandah loungers at Raffles hotel in Singapore, to waterproof capes worn in the monsoon-drenched paddy fields of China, from sweeping overhanging eaves in Thai houses to tiny split-bamboo whisks.

Oriental cane and bamboo comes from the genus *Arundinaria* and it is the largest member of the grass family. The cane used for making furniture usually comes from the rattan palms found in Southeast Asia and South America. The larger widths are used for the main construction and the smaller ones are used to wrap and strengthen the joints.

The strength of rattan, cane and wicker is exploited to the full in the structure of Thai buildings. It is used to form a lattice-work of beams lashed together to support roof and sleeping platforms, and, more prosaically, in the construction of fish-weirs and fences. The waterproof qualities of palm leaves make them a perfect thatching material, as their lightweight thickness provides a good insulation from both rain and sun. The ease with which these materials can be split and woven, or the outer casing twined and knotted means that they can be used for flooring, walls, partitions, doors, mattresses, rugs, hammocks, baskets, screens and blinds. And thriving in humid climates, they are perfectly suited to withstand those damp conditions which would make more solid building materials rot away.

The basket-making, wall- and mat-weaving that takes place in tropical regions around the world usually originates from palms. In Africa palmyra and raffia palms are used for these purposes, sometimes entirely overlaid with a decoration of cowrie shells. Nowadays, gaily coloured baskets are made in the same style, with typical ingenuity, from telephone wire.

In more temperate climates, reeds, rushes and sedges are harvested from marshland – these, along with corn husks, tend to be the favoured basket-making materials of North American Indians. The Mexicans use a coarse reed called *tule*, or brightly dyed palm, and in Mediterranean regions, esparto grass is used.

The art of basket-making goes back long before the earliest pottery, to cave dwellers in Utah, USA, some 9000 years ago. Baskets dating from *c.* 5000 BC have been found by archaeologists in Peru, woven mats found in Iraq, and basket-lined granaries uncovered in Egypt. From *c.* 1000 BC there is evidence of the so-called Basket-making Indians in New Mexico who could produce beautiful containers for storage, transport and even cooking – so finely twined and impermeable that it was possible to cook liquids in them by tossing in a heated stone.

The Californian Indians – Pomo, Hupa and Śeri – still create coiled and twined baskets of astonishing refinement, from tiny 12.5mm (1/2in) toys to watertight cooking baskets, and decorative ceremonial baskets brocaded with quail or woodpecker feathers.

A GOOD CANING
Opposite above **An amazing, almost vertically pitched roof in South Korea, made of intricately carved and gilded wood and bamboo – one way to stay cool and dry in a hot, rainy climate.**

SLEEPING NICHE
Opposite below **More fretted woodwork around an airy mosquito-curtained bed. Above it all floats a thatched roof, lined with light herringbone canework. The roof overhangs the balcony in shady eaves and the interior is further protected from the sun by split cane blinds.**

OPEN-PLAN MEXICAN
Right **An open loggia roofed in a more robust style. A coarser thatch of palapa fronds represents a sophisticated contrast to fastidious pebble-inlay floor details, rich distressed yellow walls, and a self-conscious outbreak of Rousseau-esque art on the walls. The whole structure is supported on massive tree-trunks still entwined by lianas.**

ALL ABOUT EAVES
Opposite **A somewhat claustrophobic space in the cantilevered eaves of an Indonesian house. A prevalence of cane, bamboo and rattan has been tempered by the use of pistachio green paint.**

TROPIC OF TAHITI
Right **Allusions to Gauguin enliven the walls of this house in Tahiti – the usual tropical repertoire of cane and bamboo has been artfully woven in differing patterns on walls and ceiling, and then varnished to give it a darker sheen.**

Different kinds of rattan, cane and basketry materials need different treatment. In the construction of buildings and furniture, soaking the cane in hot or cold water aids flexibility, and dry heat is sometimes used for moulding sharp corners without splitting. The hard outer skin of cane which gives it disproportionate tensile strength for its thickness, is familiar in shiny tan woven chair seats and backs, and makes tightly woven matting walls and partitions. Cane is impervious to most things, can be used indoors or out, takes paint well and weathers with dignity. Weight is a guide to the durability of cane furniture – the heavier it is, the longer it will last.

Woven cane panels and mats are easy to come by, and can be used to emulate *tatami* mats, Indonesian screens, and attached to walls and doors to give a genteel, oriental air. Seagrass, coir and jute have an earthy and hardwearing affinity with floors, and a kindly natural colour.

Hot water and soap tend to be detrimental to all these materials, and the traditional cleaning agent for rattan and cane is salt in a strong solution with cold or barely warm water, applied briskly with a scrubbing brush.

The Oriental house itself is often constructed from variants on a bamboo theme, and the elegant skeleton will be very visible, framing literally paper-thin walls. On doors and screens, lanterns and light-shades, wood may be used, but will often be reeded to look like cane. Rattan is ubiquitous in the Orient, and the respectful use of unadorned natural materials is firmly built into the Buddhist way of life. Cane is usually simply coated with shellac to make it shiny and bring out the natural markings. Fine-grained pole bamboo is steamed into shape to make furniture, and has the requisite strength to make beds and work tables. Mottled and water bamboo are the varieties that are split and woven into baskets, hats and mats.

The tools for this craft are extremely simple, consisting only of a heat source, hammer and nails, a plane with varying blade height for shaving strips for weaving and a razor-sharp curved knife with which to split the tubes. And the versatility of the material lends itself to all sorts of rather more frivolous uses, such as ornate and airy bird-cages made of ribs of split cane and bamboo umbrella frames.

PLASTER

Where the conifers end, stone, plaster and mud begin – over one third of the world's population lives in houses made of earth. Nearly three thousand years ago, the seven-storey tower of Babel was built of raw earth – and large parts of the Great Wall of China, dating from the third century BC, are still proclaiming the enduring virtues of mud. Even in France today, at least 15 per cent of rural buildings are fashioned from raw earth.

There are various different ways of making raw mud into solid architecture; two of the most common are adobe and *Pisé-de-terre*. Adobe refers to bricks of earth which may be mixed with straw, and moulded. *Pisé-de-terre* is the technique whereby thick mud walls are built by ramming wet earth into wooden frames layer by layer and removing the frames as the mud dries. These materials, basic as they are, show how to make a virtue out of necessity.

AFRICAN INLAY
Designed with all the careless confidence of a child playing with building blocks, the decoration on this pink plaster wall is patterned with inlaid chips of grey slate.

The familiar cob cottages of the southwest of England were simply clay mixed with straw and small stones piled up into massively thick walls, and plastered and limewashed for protection from the prevalent rain. Properly protected, they could last 400 years. Most mud constructions are made from a mixture of sand and clay – the clay provides the glue, and the sand the strength. Occasionally the puddled mud for the *pisé* method has exotic additives, such as palm oil for strength or waterproofing.

Rain can be a problem. The solution lies in a raised foundation of an impermeable material, such as blocks of stone, and overhanging eaves. And some sort of protective render – the Aztecs and Mesopotamians faced their buildings with stones, baked bricks or polished ceramic cones. In parts of Africa, replastering the outside of a building is an annual ceremony, accomplished with a great deal of creative energy. Minerals or vegetable extracts may be added to the basic mixture of mud and straw, and the resulting plaster may be applied in relief patterns, or smoothly coloured and polished to a reflective gloss with red earth, oil seed or locust pod extract. In more sophisticated areas the render is made up of earth mixed with bitumen or cement, which forms an efficient protective coating. And there is low-tech machinery which produces a more firmly compressed mud brick than hand-moulding can achieve. The basic process, however, is the same the world over.

Within, earth is easily sculpted and invites sinuous forays into integral furniture – seats, shelves, benches and beds which just grow out of the walls. And having felt the delicious plastic potential of putty-like mud, people just have to decorate it with impressed patterns, crimped edges, inexplicable nodules, lacy borders and runic patterns to repel the evil eye. Internal walls are often made with a mixture of mud and cow-dung – cheap, malleable and reputed to be an efficient pest repellant. Floors, too, are often made of mud and cow-dung beaten to a shiny smooth finish, and may incorporate a bright patchwork of ceramic mosaic or rounded stones, mica chips or cowrie shells.

Unbaked earth has unequalled insulating properties that recommend its use in the baking heartland of Africa and the coldest windraked mountainsides of China.

MUD RELIEF
Opposite above **Strong and simple detail that exploits the mouldable qualities of mud as a building material – a technique at which the Africans excel. The plinth is painted to match the thatch and the door makes a bright contrast.**

EARTHLY PALLOR
Opposite below **Warm, strong floor colours – consisting of terracotta tiles and bold, pink painted false skirting – make a reassuringly solid base for the airy whiteness of plaster walls and limewashed wooden ceilings in this house. The skull and the pithoi full of dead twigs lend a lugubrious air.**

CANDLE HEAT
Right **A plaster fire-hood finished with a shiny and blackened twisted log, makes a medieval-looking hearth of the most basic kind and a very simple means of heating a room.**

AL FRESCO SEAT
Opposite **An unexpected and artistic collection of colours decorates this inviting corner – a transparent mauve wash on the rough plaster walls is complemented by woodwork, dry brushed with verdigris and outlined with salmon-pink round the window. It is the translucency of the different colours that makes them work so well together.**

PLASTER LACEWORK
Right **A bedroom in a very organic house in Tunisia, which has the air of having been hewn from a rock-face – the filigree shelves are an extension of the mud walls, and pieces of ceramic have been incorporated into the bed-base.**

STAMPED STUCCO
Far right **Casual patterns stamped in wet plaster and then washed with terracotta paint. The demarcation line between two days' work is visible but does not detract from the richness of effect. The pink works particularly well with dusty black and white floor tiles.**

Mud and earth are not only a practical answer to cheap houses – they are materials which can produce buildings of a rounded, user-friendly sculptural beauty unequalled by any other methods. They adapt to all kinds of embellishment, whether it be three-dimensional, painted, or a Gaudi-esque mosaic of bright ceramic chips. In India, leaves are pressed into the wet plaster, leaving an outline of delicate veining. Lacy bands of fretted openwork, concentric niches to house a local deity, pillars, pointed crenellations, swirling raised patterns as complex as soutache braid frogging, delicate borders and arches as refined as piped icing – this is all kid's stuff to the experienced practitioner in mud.

For those of us who find mud and cow-dung a little hard to come by, or who suffer from an inexplicable attack of squeamishness, shovel raised over a cow-pat in mid-field, there are alternatives for achieving a look of rough hand-hewn plaster using PVA-bound (polyvinyl acetate) smooth-texture coating applied roughly with brush and plasterer's trowel. It helps to seal the wall initially with a coat of PVA mixed with an equal volume of water, important if you want to use an oil-based paint. Or an experienced plasterer can give life to cement, lime and sand plaster, by working over the top coat with a cross-grained wood float, just as the plaster begins to dry.

For a three-dimensional design on the exterior of plastered buildings, there are professional pargetters who can produce traditional designs at the drop of a hat. Pargetting is a technique usually confined to quaintly uneven thatched cottages in East Anglia, by which regular designs are stamped with patterned wood blocks or combed into the soft rough plaster. There is no reason why stamped and moulded designs should not decorate interior walls, applied quickly to a slow-drying skim-coat. To be utterly authentic, you would insist on a mixture of equal parts of clay, lime and cow-dung, with chopped straw as a reinforcing agent.

Tinted limewash is a lively finish for rough plaster, and has the quality of discouraging noxious wildlife. Use it over existing emulsion paint as long as you seal it first with size.

Where the local geology throws up rock and stone, this will be reflected in the choice of building material – if not the entire building, then details and structural aspects such as fireplaces, kitchen and bathroom fittings, quoins, lintels and arches are likely to take advantage of its doughty good looks and durability. Granite is synonymous with toughness, and the walls of granite buildings survive long after the more ephemeral roof and timbers have rotted away, though their aspect tends to be dour, and some say damp within. Sandstone and limestone tend to weather and decay, and need a fair amount of care and cosseting.

In rural England cob, witchit, chalk or clay lump – all names for earth as a building material – used to be dug straight from the ground. It was then spread over an area in a layer 30 cm (1 ft) thick, watered and mixed with straw and trodden or 'tempered' by horse, ox or men. At this point chalk, sand or gravel, or even broken slate were added to give strength. The puddled material was then built into thick walls on a base of pebbles or brick, or occasionally shaped into large blocks roughly the size and shape of breeze-blocks, and left to dry for several months. A painfully slow procedure.

Stone is speedier, but more intractable, particularly the more ancient igneous rock types, such as granite, slatestone, lava and tufa. These are rock types which are synonymous with immutability, as one can deduce from the jagged, barely-shaped blocks of the walls of granite houses. There is a doughty masculinity about rough-hewn stone which suits unpretentious interiors, in moderation, as it does gale-blasted bothy walls. It is often used in rural France, Italy and Spain for fireplaces and sinks, sculptural stairs, textured interior walls and time-worn floors, sophisticated carved plinths and pilasters, niches and architectural details, even occasionally massive and horrendously heavy baths.

Stone is one of those appealing materials that improves with age and hard wear. Floors are polished by the passage of innumerable feet, sinks and drainers smoothed by decades of scrubbing. Damp sawdust and a stiff brush are the most practical tools for cleaning stone floors; marble and stone should not be left wet as they may suffer salt-marks.

RUGGED BAROQUE
Opposite above
Chunky masculine surfaces, as roughly hewn as they come, in curious contrast with a curly mirror and frilly lightshade. Colours and textures of wood, stone and plaster work harmoniously together to produce a bathroom which, despite not being exactly user-friendly, is pleasing to the eye.

ITALIAN ELEGANCE
Opposite below **The peasanty plainness of this stone sink is elegantly contradicted by its curvaceous pedestal. A king's ransom of pewter plates decks the shelves above, along with more utilitarian pans.**

PLASTER DISTRESSED
Left **In fact, plaster almost undone – here the effect is so venerably antiqued, so worn with age, so spider-trodden and mildewed, chipped and flaked and damp-stained, that one can only applaud its audacity.**

PAINT

For walls, woodwork and furniture, paint is the cosmetic *par excellence*. The simple magic of colour and texture effects transformations like nothing else can, and crops up in the most unlikely places. In the south of Ireland for instance, among the grey pebbledash bungalows, there may suddenly burst a shot of pure unadulterated colour – walls and woodwork in competing primaries defying the rain to do its worst and refusing to submit to the grey skies. And among the polite farmsteads of rural Denmark, there are buildings of extravagant brightness; a variety of vivid colours including rich red, moss green and copper.

Where the sun burns brightly and predictably the year round, in the Caribbean, Haiti, India and Africa, a pauper's wealth of colour is celebrated and everyone can achieve the effect they desire quite simply with a bright splash of paint.

GUATEMALAN BOLD
Shocking pink and aquamarine is a daring combination, enhanced by the slightly textured translucency of the paint.

SHELF-EXPRESSION
Above Stippled walls, eggbox frills and a little light relief in an African shelving unit.

PAINTED PORTALS
Opposite top left Extrovert colours in Agadir.
Opposite top right Variants on black, blue and white on a doorway in Tunisia.
Opposite bottom left A tiny bright shutter painted in soft luminous colours.
Opposite bottom right Minimal decoration and maximum impact on door and wall in Guadeloupe.

Colour, used imaginatively and slapped on in jazzy contrasts of tone and shade, draws attention to relief patterns and door details and can be painted on in geometric shapes or bold outlines. The chalky paint, applied in an amazing array of colours that one sees on rough Greek and Turkish cement and plaster walls and sparkling under tropical palms in the Caribbean has now trickled through to cooler climes. People under grey skies are now painting their houses pistachio green, aqua or ice-cream pink with specially imported Turkish paint.

On the outside of many ethnic buildings, doors and windows are particularly emphasized, framed with rows of pattern painted freehand or applied with a block (cut in sponge or polystyrene for uneven walls), or with architectural details like the elaborately carved wooden window surrounds of Russian buildings shown off with strong colour counterpoint. Almost without exception made of wood, external doors have to be hardwearing, to withstand weather and the depredations of children, dogs, bicycles or whatever else needs to cross the threshold. The doors themselves may have a *trompe l'oeil* design of studs and ornate hinges, an intricate Islamic interlaced pattern, or the simple expedient of using bright cerulean blue against snowy whitewash, beloved of the Greeks. Specialist paint companies have historic and traditional colours ready mixed to suit sober Shaker or Williamsburg American, subdued Scandinavian colour schemes or the strong blues, greens and sandy reds of Moroccan tiles and paintwork.

Limewash in some form or other is an almost universal exterior wall paint, and it takes kindly to tinting, producing luminous and lively colour. Its caustic content means that it has mild disinfecting properties. By allowing the surface to 'breathe' it can to some extent obviate the need for a damp-proof course. This breathing quality is a much-prized aspect of the new generation of ecology friendly paints, which have now come full circle, and have jettisoned the discoveries of the modern plastics and petroleum industries in favour of the old-fashioned methods and natural ingredients.

Paint effects are among the oldest, most versatile crafts. From walls and ceilings to furniture and picture frames a touch of the exotic can be added very simply. Distemper is the indoor equivalent of limewashing, but has the disadvantage that it must be washed off surfaces before repainting. Colourwashing with different shades of watered-down emulsion, or sponging on emulsion can emulate the lively broken colour of traditional paint finishes. Fine detail, indoors or out, is easiest applied in water-based paints such as acrylic or PVA paint which dry fast and do not run, and are then sealed with wax or matt varnish. If you are copying complex painted panels to apply to a matt ground, it is sometimes useful to make a slide of the original, and project it onto the area to be painted, so that you can sketch the outlines straight on the wall. Refer back to the original transparency if any problems arise. For a look of antiquity and authenticity, it is often a good idea to gently distress the object or woodwork to be painted, and then to tint the sealing varnish with raw or burnt umber, raw or burnt sienna, a little rottenstone or to use a crackle glaze.

The bright, unmuddied colours of Oriental painting, and their complexity of pattern, are quite difficult to achieve, though red lacquer or black japanning can be successfully faked. Prepare the surface to a silky smoothness with sanded gesso then polish off with shellac mixed with half as much methylated spirit. For red lacquer, mix vermilion artist's oil colour with a little white spirit and flat white oil-based paint. Give the object three coats of this, sanding carefully in between. Then apply two coats of gloss varnish mixed with a squeeze of crimson and burnt sienna artist's oil paint. Tone down if necessary with a final glaze of transparent burnt umber.

Black japanning is easier, though your flat black oil-based paint could be enriched by a squeeze of burnt umber. Sand between coats as before. For the two final coats mix the black paint and burnt umber with a dollop of gloss varnish. Finish off with two coats of polyurethane gloss varnish warmed by a dab of burnt umber artist's oil paint. Polish the final coat with rottenstone, wax and buff well. With lacquer, unfortunately, perfection is what you are after, and no less than seven coats will do. And of course

MUTED WOOD
Opposite The rough and cracked planks of a Scandinavian timber house incorporate hand-painted runic swirls of grey on cream.

FLORAL SHUTTERS
Above left Intricate matt paintwork on a pair of Moroccan shutters.

RAINBOW CEILING
Above right A Tibetan temple boasts a stepped wooden ceiling on which dragons chase pearls.

rigorous sanding down and wiping in between, since the slightest blip will show. Stencilling and gilding with metallic powder can further embellish this rich and luscious finish.

The panelled wooden interiors of some Oriental houses are painted in gleaming lacquer, window frames fluently ragged with russet, panels dragged and then quickly drawn with jagged blossom-laden branches and chrysanthemums. The effect is rich, controlled and impossible to emulate, as bosses of temple beams in Tibet, whose stylized flowers and scrolls would be ridiculous elsewhere, have a jewel-like richness in their proper place.

Naive painted wooden furniture and tongued-and-grooved timber panelling gains considerable depth and interest painted and finished this way – prepare the wood with a coat of French enamel varnish thinned with twice its volume of methylated spirit. When it has dried, paint it with a coat of emulsion, followed by a thinner coat of toning emulsion diluted with three times as much water. Different intensities of rust reds, blue and green, sage green and greenish pearwood, Venetian red and olive green, make good partnerships which have a sympathy to wood. Sand the paint back, especially where you might expect worn areas, and seal with varnish or beeswax. Casein paint can be used in the same way, and sanded back. It has a matt finish that 'ages' gracefully, but is durable at the same time. It is also possible to stencil on any type of painted surface provided it is clean. If you have used gloss paint, a coat of matt varnish will make the stencil easier to apply. If you are applying the stencil to natural wood, make sure to seal it with matt or satin varnish.

Gloss paint gives great weather protection and in strong rich colours is favoured for the rainbow woodwork of the Caribbean. There is a move towards using the slightly more interesting casein paints traditional to Shaker architecture or the linseed oil and zinc paints used in Scandinavia for external woodwork. Natural, non-toxic, mostly plant-based paints are now available and are a refreshing alternative in our over-sophisticated world, and these, tinted with vegetable and mineral extracts have the great advantage of effortless colour harmony – without harsh aniline and chemical dyes, it is positively difficult to get colours to clash.

CRISP BLACK AND WHITE
Opposite above **Exterior of a cottage in the Solca region of Romania. The decoration in white is pre-marked in smooth plaster against the rough render of the surrounding black wall, and the matt paint is very opaque, both on wall and window-frame.**

WEDDING PICTURE
Opposite below **The brightest of primary colours, red predominating, are used for this Transylvanian wedding portrait, painted by the bride's mother on the panelled wood of a built-in storage unit. The dark sludgy green is made from the black and yellow mixed together.**

WELL SPOTTED
Left **An unusual American decorative technique that dates from the seventeenth century. Loved by some and loathed by others, it offers a strange combination of light-hearted spottiness and rather serious dark woodwork.**

TEXTILES

Textiles can be used as portable decoration, furniture and sometimes homes. In practical terms, textiles can be transformed into walls, floor, ceiling and window coverings and beds. They may also provide seating, warmth and shade. In symbolic terms they may proclaim wealth, weddings, dowries or death. Ethnic textiles tend by definition to be on the low-tech scale of production. Using available materials and employing traditional techniques, evolved over centuries, pieces are produced to a high degree of artistic refinement. They are used to transform public into private, banal into theatrical, and to infuse magic into the quotidian business of life. Textiles can be bone-simple and functional, but given the overpowering urge to decorate, they are more likely to be coloured, embroidered, trimmed, printed or embellished in some way to celebrate the wonderful inventiveness of the human spirit.

RED MOROCCO
A chance meeting between a red Moroccan woven rug, and a crumbling plastered wall of similar intense colour.

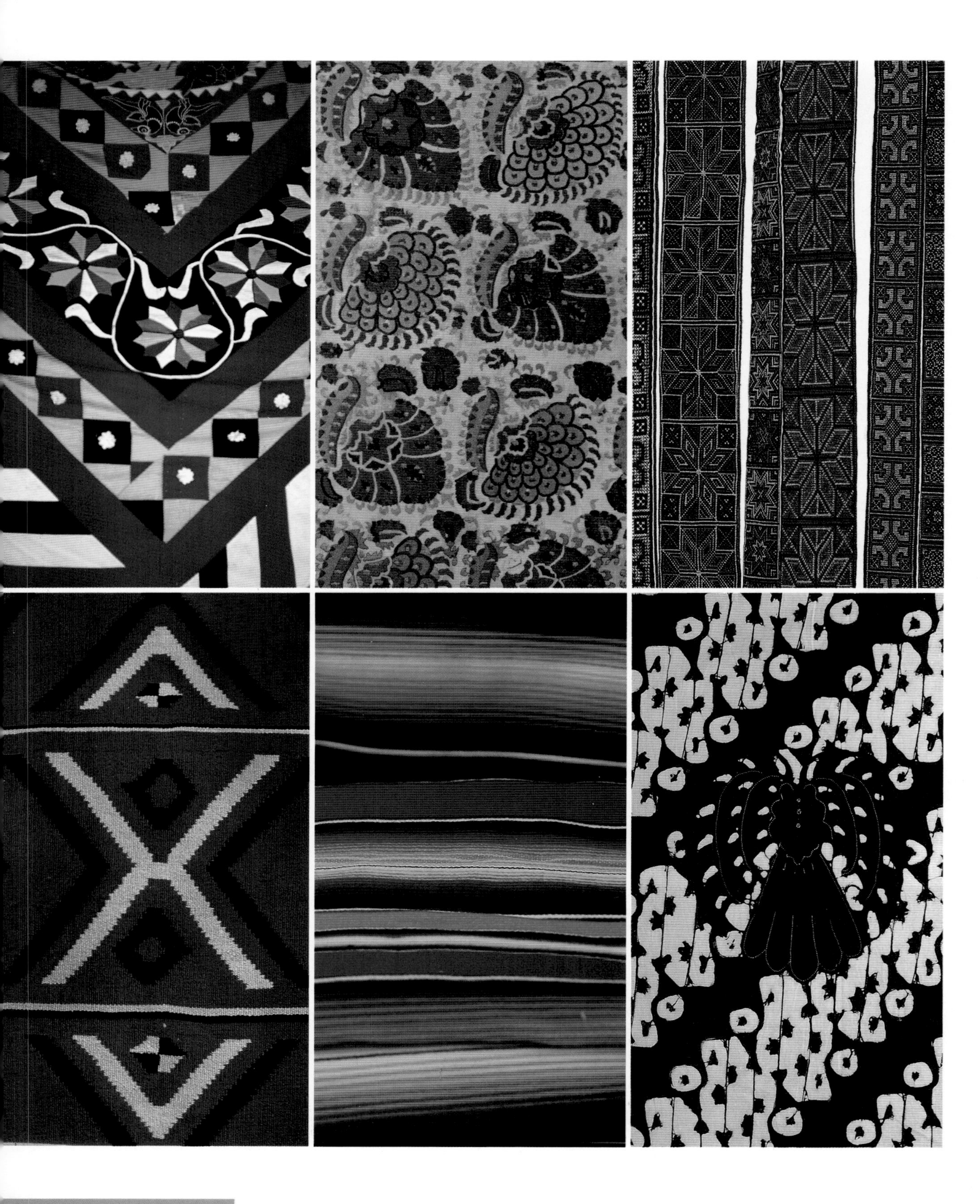

THE FABRIC OF SOCIETY
Top left **A bold Brazilian appliquéd quilt.**
Top centre **A regular formation of exuberant stylized flowers embroidered on a late seventeenth-century Turkish textile.**
Top right **Strips of woven sash fabric from Thailand.**
Bottom left **A Navajo rug woven in the traditional way from a trio of clean, sharp colours.**
Bottom centre **Impossible brilliance of colour in a Mexican blanket from the Yucatan.**
Bottom right **Fine cotton wax-resist batik from Jogjakavta in brown and black on a white ground.**
Opposite **A flat-woven woollen Afghanistan kelim bordered by a variant of the tree pattern.**

Textiles express the character of the world from which they come – the batik of Indonesia is laden with tradition, there are classic designs to which names are assigned – *nam kepang* is a striped herringbone, *tirta teja* is a stepped chevron, the *naga* is a familiar grinning dragon of which there are many variations. Even the manufacturing tools – the fine spouted canting with which the oil is applied, and the carved wooden stamps – have a certain grace and beauty, and a serenely introverted method of production. By contrast, Fijian barkcloth is made communally, and the process is a rhythmic, jolly, noisy one, consisting of beating strips of bark with wooden mallets against a log, and the whole procedure takes place out-of-doors in a sociable gaggle.

Backstrap looms, where the tension of the warp is achieved by the weaver simply straining against the loom with his or her back, are almost universal, and can produce strips of cloth of utter simplicity or in sophisticated weaves – Indonesian weavers can produce richly brocaded tapestry fabrics, while in Guatemala, Peru and Mexico the impact tends to come from vibrant combinations of colour in lively stripes. The portable nature of the backstrap loom means that the subtle art of weaving can continue in a land riven by war, and in Guatemala, helicopters and guns have replaced fertility motifs in a silent plea for help and as despairing documentation of violent times.

Indian textiles are the most complex and richly worked of any, and a single – usually deeply symbolic – hanging may combine tie-dye, printing, embroidery, mirror-work, patchwork and appliqué in a blinding mosaic of colour whose function may be to repel the evil eye and send it reeling from the door. In India, textiles are used with unusual ingenuity and are adapted for all sorts of purposes. They are hung up to make 'cupboard' fronts and room dividers; they embellish shrines and doors, food safes and shelves, thereby investing the most banal aspects of life with dignity.

Navajo and Pueblo rugs have a strongly graphic character, and a confident artistry with a limited palette of red, black, indigo and cream (with occasional forays into more subtle greens and pinks) which is the perfect partner to the butch bare wood and white-painted adobe of West Coast and central American homes.

In Egypt, loud traditional patchwork hangings are made into *ad hoc* rooms, awnings or enclosures wherever a spot of shade or privacy is wanted; similarly swirls and curlicues on appliquéd quilts create exotic tents in which Polynesian weddings take place; among the nomadic Berbers, tent-hangings and rugs make a patch of desert into an instant home, bringing warmth, colour and familiarity to a strange place. The entrance to the tent may have a symbolic embroidered flap, and within, precious possessions are protected by richly embroidered carrying cloths. On the other side of the world, a brilliant rainbow-striped hammock makes a portable Mexican bed. In India, instant ceremonial significance is awarded to ordinary rooms by hanging a gaily pennanted *toran* or a *ganesh* embroidered with a gaggle of gods and complete with devil-defying mirror fragments above a door, or a *ras mandel* wedding canopy with its central solar disc over the ceiling and a gaudily embroidered wedding mat on the floor. Appliquéd banners in Africa extol a man's military exploits and paint his pedigree, whereas indigo and white-striped hangings outside the door tell passers-by of a death within.

Simple flatwoven cotton – unbleached calico, canvas or muslin – is an adaptable and good-natured fabric, still cheap, hardwearing, and handsome in generous quantities. The strength and elasticity of cotton are due to its spiral structure, unique among natural fibres. It fades with gentility and being practical and easily cared for, is well suited to an outdoor life on verandahs, hammocks, awnings and blinds.

Woven stripes are the next level of complication, of which the startlingly brilliant striped textiles of Mexico and Guatemala are the most stunning. Very simple, often still woven by hand on a primitive backstrap loom from cotton (or wool), they continue an ancient tradition of Mayan artistry with dye.

The most glorious ethnic printed fabrics are the stamped black *adinkra* funeral cloth of Ghana, the cassava-paste resist-indigo and white *adire eleko* cloth of Nigeria, the patterns and paisleys from India, particularly the Rajasthan region, and the wax resist hand-decorated Javanese Batik *tulis*, all of which combine exquisite artistry in pattern and colour with a fresh spontaneity of finish.

SIMPLE CURTAINS
Opposite **An open verandah in Bangkok, which can be curtained off for privacy and shade. Simple folds of heavy plain cotton hang well, and do not break the bank; silk is even better, but does prove expensive.**

BRIGHT TEXTILES
Above right **This Marrakesh interior would lose much without the textiles – the room is casually enclosed by a broad sweep of palest pink cotton; the brick floor is warmed by the black and white dhurrie; and the red tablecloth combines all the decorative elements, bringing the whole interior to life.**

WATERSIDE LOUNGING
Above far right **A sumptuous view of hills and water in India, a soft mountain of gold and white cushions, a flask of wine, and the company of just about anyone – a perfect recipe for the good life.**

HANGING AROUND
Below right **A hammock of cotton and crocheted lace overlooks a colourburst of geraniums on an Ibizan verandah.**

Embroidery is a means of embellishment for household textiles and clothing much favoured in India, the Middle East and the Baltic region.

In Czechoslovakia, modest homes have a riotously bright and embroidered corner, where friendly ancestral spirits might enter the house on feast days. Other traditional sites for embroidery with symbolic intent are light-sources such as candlesticks, windows and mirrors, the cooking stove, and washbasins which merit decoration because of the symbolic power of water. These will be hung with cloths bearing cult motifs of pairs of birds, initials or the tree of life.

Doors and thresholds, marriage and childbirth beds (beautiful bed-tents in Greece are common) are often hung with embroidered cloths to protect the inhabitants, similar to the L-shaped *sankhia* hangings of Saurashtra.

In Uzbekistan, finely worked embroidered rugs, silk on cotton, covered in flowers and geometric shapes and looking very like American patchwork quilts, are an essential part of a girl's dowry. And in India a family's embroidered quilts may be so numerous as to form a tall polychrome stack, hidden behind yet another embroidered hanging known as a *dharaniyo*.

In Greece, the women of the family used to embroider a dowry consisting of linens, blankets, rugs and bed-hangings. The stitches used tended to be simple running-stitch, satin-stitch and cross-stitch variants, and the opulence of the finished article relied on the rich colour and sheen of the silk embroidery floss on plain white or cream linen. The silk was home grown and then dyed in plant or bark colouring or the red dye from the kermes insect.

Second to cotton, wool is the most familiar fibre among household textiles throughout the world, and from prehistoric times has served for blankets and floor coverings. In the Near East, the source of so many glorious carpet styles, woollen carpet weaving began in the eleventh century, and the tradition of using natural dyes, in closely guarded secret formulae, continued until the advent of chemical dyes in the second half of the nineteenth century. Previously, madder and indigo, berries, plants, fruit, bark and fungi were the main constituents, and the colours they produced were liable to local variation dictated by the qualities of the water used.

AN AIRY THRONE
Opposite above
Exaggerated fringes give an unconvincing touch of softness to a spartan day-bed, and serve also to diminish slightly the disproportionate height of this room.

STRIPES AND SKULLS
Opposite below
Brilliant Mexican blankets, all different, make the simplest of curtains and marry two quite different window styles. Lavender paint on chest and walls gives coherence too.

WOVEN DIAMONDS
Right **Variations on diamonds and chevrons from ceiling to floor in a tall airy North African room. An object lesson in how to make the simplest elements – the squares and blocks of colour familiar from nursery school – combine in texture and harmony both rich and sophisticated. Strong earth and sunset shades relate beautifully in a contemporary kelim used as a dramatic wallhanging, squared patchwork tablecloth and finely woven rug. The inlaid chair and lacy fretwork screen soften a severely rectilinear room.**

PHILADELPHIA MIXTURE
Left **An eclectic collection of the best of American folk style. This bedroom is dominated by a bold patchwork and appliqué quilt together with Shakerish gingham curtains on bedrail and window. Plain calico bed-hangings contribute to an overwhelming feeling of calm, conducive to sweet dreams.**

NORWEGIAN SIMPLE
Opposite **Coarse cotton weaving acts as insulation on box beds and floor. The dark cobalt tongued-and-grooved walls make a sympathetic background to the nicely detailed pine, allowing the character of the wood to dominate; the room is finished off with the ubiquitous woven runner.**

North African and Persian rugs are famous for their stained glass brilliance of colour and floral geometric filigree design. Among the nomads, knotted rugs are made, and in Morocco and Tunisia cruder, but no less desirable flat-weave kelims are woven in soft colours with stylized animal motifs.

Woollen Navajo flat-weave serapes from Arizona were made from the 1700s onwards as clothing and bedding. Initially and traditionally, they were woven from undyed yarn in shades of black, brown and white, with the addition of a few native dyes. Indigo came from Europe in the early 1800s, and English-made red baize was imported, carefully unravelled and incorporated in weavings as the ubiquitous bayeta red. At the beginning of the century, the Navajo began to produce the bright and beautiful floor rugs that are an essential accoutrement to any well-dressed Central American home. New Mexican *jerga* rugs are simpler and more basic, thickly woven in narrow strips to cope with uneven and rocky floors. They tend to be indigo, red and yellow woven into plaids, stripes or checks.

In North America the thrifty rural tradition is for naive pictorial hooked rugs on a jute backing, sometimes using a commercially stencilled design (Edward Sands Frost of Maine initiated this idea in the late nineteenth century, followed speedily by mail-order firms), and worked painstakingly over the snowbound winter months. Rag rugs were also hooked, knitted, crocheted or plaited from scraps. They tended not to be fine art, and their biodegradable composting qualities have been wryly praised by their creators. In the passion for decoration evinced by the busy ladies of North America, plain sail canvas or heavy duck floorcloths were painted and stencilled too in New England to add colour to bare wooden boards.

In Poland, Romania and Scandinavia there is a penchant for long narrow rugs, flat-woven from wool, with a cotton, hemp or flax warp. In Romania these are known as *scoarta*, meaning tree-bark, because bark was once used to line the walls of peasant houses, and the rugs initially replaced this function. The tiny geometric figures – chain mail, tablets, little mouth, eyelets, starlets were some of their names – bear a strong resemblance to Scandinavian *ryiji* rugs with their pots of flowers, figures and animals.

They were originally used for protection and warmth for fishermen in their small open boats. In Sweden, rugs were given to couples as wedding presents – forming a little island depicting a man and a woman holding hands upon which the couple stood to be married, or knotted pile rugs with floral designs with which they covered the marriage bed. Long flat-weave runners are the standard Scandinavian floor finish, familiar from the watercolours of Carl Larsson, bringing a touch of life and imparting warmth and colour to bare wood.

And in the most wild, inaccessible and inhospitable places in the world the finest and most precious wools are grown – in the Himalayas a particular breed of tough, hardy goat produces cashmere (a highly prized fashion accessory in the West). In Peru and the high, cold places of South America, the fine silky pelt of the alpaca and the vicuna is sheared and woven or knitted into necessary insulation against the cold – parkas, rugs and sleeping bags.

GREEK FINERY
Opposite **An ingenious platform bedroom/sitting-room, with an example of just about every Greek textile, from *flokati* to cutwork lace, embroidery to flatweave rugs and coarse cotton woven stripes.**

SHEER LUXURY
Above left **The perfect vantage point from which to observe the street without being seen, hidden behind seductive folds of semi-transparent voile.**

TENTED SPLENDOUR
Above right **An extraordinary umbrella of printed silk floating above a huge circular North African room.**

CROSS-STITCH AND TRINKETS
Below right **A still life with embroidered poppies and cornflowers, a row of rose-strewn handkerchiefs making a matching border at a shrine to family history.**

CERAMICS

Ceramics take their name from the Greek word for earthenware and have been around for thousands of years. From their Egyptian origins in the fourth millennium BC when blue-glazed bricks were used to build houses, to the Greek traditions of highly sophisticated shaped clay, the craft has spread wide throughout the world. Traditional designs have remained unchanged through the ages, for example the swirling, earth-brown motifs produced by the Navajo Indians and the bucolic scenes of chirpy peasant life represented on Delft tiles. In Japan, the clay is unadorned, save for a calligraphic swash in muted colours. In Italy and Spain, the same play provides the excuse for an explosion of majolica, an intricate rainbow of colour and pattern brought to life by contrast with a plain white ground. As common denominator to it all lies the influence of the Orient – not for nothing is our tableware known as china.

RANDOM PATCHWORK
A patio in Provence, its floor tiled in a typical mixture of glazed greens, blues, orange, cream and terracotta, earthy colours well partnered by the discreet grey-blue of the paintwork and gently rusting furniture.

In the Middle East, influenced by the Chinese, the tradition for tiles flowered. T'ang porcelain found its way to Mesopotamia in the middle of the eighth century, and local potters set about trying to emulate the delicate white porcelain – unsuccessfully, but in experimenting managed to create a very different ceramic art of their own which consisted in covering buff earthenware with an opaque white glaze, which they then embellished by painting on transparent lead glazes in blue and green.

In the ninth century came the discovery of lustre; pottery designs became more and more intricate, and included relief-patterned champlevé tiles, occasionally decorated with Kufic inscriptions. In the thirteenth century, Persian potters began to perfect underglaze and overglaze painting, with crisp definition and as many as seven colours, cobalt blue, turquoise and black predominating. Everyone started to want tiles, and they began to be produced for humbler abodes than palaces and mosques, in a patchwork of interlocking shapes dictated by the passion for mathematical order that directed the genius of Islam – stars, crosses, hexagons, squares and rectangles all fitted together with immaculate precision.

In the fourteenth century the Persians were busy again, this time producing three-dimensional carved tiles to imitate stucco, with an intricate complexity of inscriptions, arabesques and geometric motifs glazed in brilliant colours – blue, green, purple and yellow. In the second half of the fourteenth century the Alhambra in Granada was completed as a magnificent Moorish stronghold, and entirely faced with small geometric tiles, *alicatados,* in soft colours of olive green, grey-blue, black, cinnamon brown and yellow.

The fortress/palace of the Alhambra with its *muqarnas*, ubiquitous stalactites of wood and plaster, its tiles and richly carved plaster pay homage to a passion for ornate floral decoration and mathematical symmetry – a narrow repertoire which attests to the Islamic prohibition against portraying 'graven images' – human or animal forms. Astonishing encrustations of arabesques and intertwining strapwork are the sublime expression of a style familiar throughout North Africa, Portugal, southern Spain, and more flamboyantly, in Spanish America.

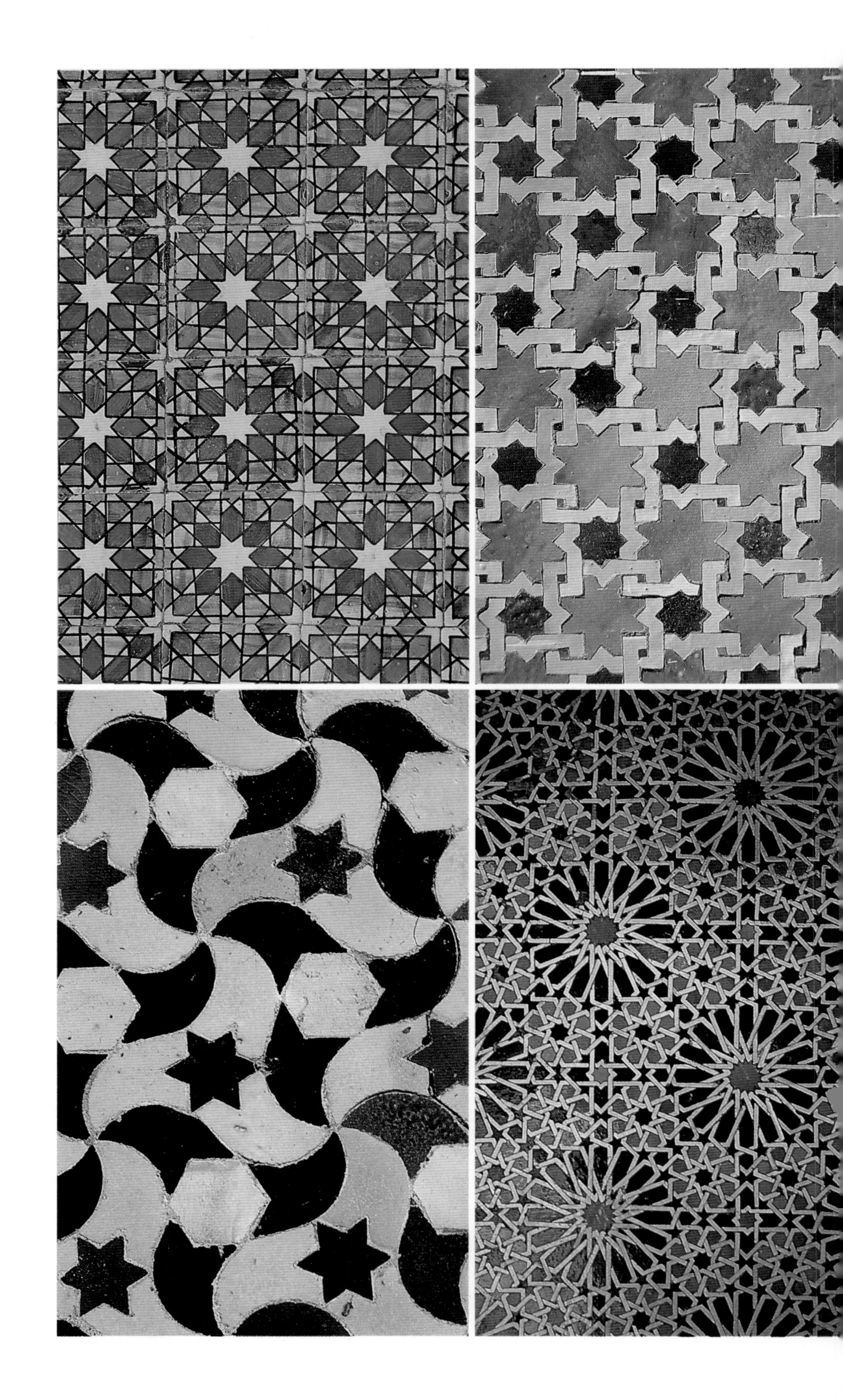

INTERNATIONAL STARS
Opposite top left **Painted glazed Portuguese tiles from La Pena demonstrate a timeless design.**
Opposite top right **A jigsaw of shaped glazed solid colour tiles from North Africa echo the star shapes from Portugal.**
Opposite below left **Freeform-shaped mosaic tiles in the Alhambra, Granada, show a strong Moorish influence.**
Opposite below right **The look to which other tiles aspire – the perfect expression of refinement and delicacy in complex mosaic tiles from Morocco.**

FLOORED GENIUS
Right **A perfect geometry of cobalt and white tiles beautifully contrasted with soft terracotta walls, in Marrakesh. The overall effect is dramatic without being stark and the choice of materials and colours is warm and inviting providing a thoroughly durable and practical solution which highlights and defines the space without taking over.**

CRISP DEFINITION
Top left **A tiny window, deeply recessed into thick walls, with a neat border of small hand-made blue and white tiles, is the perfect counterpoint to the warmth of terracotta.**

FIRED EARTH
Bottom left **A small room, dwarfed by a vast fireplace, contains a dramatic floor made up of a stunning patchwork of bright tiles.**

TILE FANATICS
Opposite **Mexico and Portugal share a wild obsession with tiles, using them with profligate generosity inside and out – this Mexican kitchen is a chequerboard of worn and dignified brown and white. Easy to clean, the effect is warm and homely while being both hygienic and bold to look at.**

Nowadays, a rich border of tiles is an essential feature to mark the grave rite of passage at a doorway. A Moorish doorway will usually have one of the traditional four arches – horseshoe-shaped, pointed, rounded Roman or the complex many-lobed bite and will be tiled in a multiplicity of colour and pattern. Within, the senses are soothed by a private paradise, cloistered courtyards cooled with an expanse of tiles, watered occasionally to keep the temperature down, and the tranquil sound of water will bubble from a central fountain surrounded by flowers, herbs and orange trees. *Muskin*, one of the Arabic names for home, comes from the same root as *sakun*, meaning peace.

The Italians, by contrast, are masters of bright and colourful majolica, vividly painted with heraldic devices, portraiture, mottoes and symbolic motifs, in a wide variety of shapes – circles, lozenges, hexagons, triangles, as well as the more predictable squares and rectangles. Religious persecution drove a handful of majolica artists as far north as The Netherlands in the late sixteenth century, and through this exodus, combined with other influences, blue and white Delft tiles eventually evolved, as the familiar decorative and hygienic solution to kitchen, dairy, hall and cellar walls, and tiled chimneys. As these Dutch potters travelled, the style also became popular throughout Northern Europe.

The Portuguese were busy with Indian-inspired tile designs, known as *azulejos*, with which they encased the exteriors of buildings.

Spanish tilemakers travelled to Mexico in the seventeenth century, taking the majolica technique with them. The style was there transformed into a frisky and insouciant patchwork known as *puebla*. In Latin America, tiles are second nature, and are spattered generously on every available surface. They are cool, easy to clean, and put together with no petty restraints of economy or perfectionist pattern making. Glazed tiles in unabashed combinations of scarlet, emerald, buttercup yellow and crudely patterned blue and white embellish pillared and niched church porticoes with all the extrovert unselfconsciousness of a child with poster paints. Vigorous mixtures of pattern and colour explode on humble interior walls with a naive charm that would be difficult to emulate in our more deliberate *modus operandi*.

Northern European lead-, tin- and salt-glazed tiles in hearty peasant style, or decorated with variants of the Delft theme continued to be made for floors and walls as well as the ubiquitous tiled stove. From Black Forest Germany they were exported widely and introduced to America as part of the Pennsylvania 'Dutch' (bastardization of Deutsch) cargo.

Tile-patterned walls are familiar in Mediterranean countries and South America. Delicate hand-painted tiles are the standard finish for the huge and regal stoves that dominate Scandinavian interiors, and are traditional for kitchens, dairies, halls, and skirtings in Holland, which gave its name to the blue and white bucolic idylls immortalized in Delft tiles. In Friesland it was usual to have a multicoloured vase of flowers depicted in tiles placed behind the family cooking range in the kitchen.

Floors of terracotta and tiles, brick and slate, stone and even marble have a traditional air, and age gracefully. The tiles are hardwearing, the colours are warm and the touch is cool. Mediterranean and North African interiors are kept cool by dousing the floor with water from time to time, and these waterproof flooring materials have always been favoured for the messy business of cooking and washing – kitchens, bathrooms and places where hygiene is paramount. Dairies for example, are typically floored with a shining expanse of tiles.

Quarry tiles have an intrinsic variation in colour and size, which is part of their appeal. They are best left unpolished and unsealed, their natural beauty brought out by the classic expedient of boiled linseed oil and turpentine – the same mixture in quantities of one to four will enhance the chilly charms of slate too. Stone and terracotta can be sealed with varnish or sealer, or burnished with wax to bring out the natural colour. Bricks and clay paviors can be left to their own devices, as can ceramic tiles, but it pays to ascertain that tiles can cope with heavy-duty use on floors before purchasing them in quantity. Originally used in grand medieval buildings, the Victorians revived tiles and, influenced by Pugin and Morris, used them widely. Encaustic floor tiles are one of the most distinctive features of nineteenth-century interiors, particularly in hallways. You can find originals in architectural salvage yards.

BORDER SKIRMISHES
Above left **Everything here is firmly bordered in a mixture of finishes – carved stone, trellis, panelling, fretwork. The strong tile design acts as a disciplined common denominator and gives coherence to the distinctly separate elements.**

COOL PRACTICALITY
Below left **This rustic Spanish bathroom with its tiny spyhole window has handsome terracotta on the floor and delicate blue and red diamond-patterned tiles on the wall.**

TILE CONSCIOUS
Opposite **From the stone slabs on the floor to the Delft on the walls, this is an interior dedicated to tiles – an excess which is nicely controlled by the severity of the dark green woodwork in the kitchen, and uplifted by the uneven ceramic patchwork in the dining room.**

The kindred arts of three-dimensional pottery have had a strong folk tradition – regional styles have sprung up all over the world, with each local identity proclaimed in its pottery decoration. For example, among the five basic North American Indian pottery-making areas, there were originally at least 40 different styles.

In Mexico, pottery was being produced a millennium before the birth of Christ, and subsequently found expression in thousands of different objects serving purposes as diverse as jewellery, funerary urns, musical instruments and temple roof ornaments. Every home has a panoply of arcane cooking accoutrements – water jars, a flat griddle for cooking tortillas, a bowl-shaped grater called a *molcajete*, and *pichanchas* – colanders for straining the maize. The most dramatic of this vernacular pottery is the glossy pitch black of the round-bellied pots produced in the oxygen-starved kilns of San Bartolo Coyotepec, which reduce the red iron oxide of the raw material to black.

The Japanese and Chinese are the masters of utterly simple utilitarian glazed ware, occasionally enlivened with the merest splash of casual hand-painting that boasts an enviable fluent elegance. Everyone must be familiar with casual rustic blue and white Chinese fish bowls, and in a more urbane tradition, the sleek unadorned rectangular dishes used by the Japanese to show off their jewel-like food. Just as Japanese wood carvers and carpenters believe that every tree wants to live again, it seems that every Japanese potter wishes to breathe life back into clay – the minimal surface decoration of ordinary everyday pottery serves to enhance the natural material, and draw attention to the subtleties of colour and texture already present. Not for them the excesses of Italian polychrome majolica, or the paintbox-bright fake fruit beloved of the Mexicans.

Spain, Portugal and Italy are the sources for a more light-hearted and purely decorative approach to pottery. Wayside shops sell mounds of terracotta containers in shapes refined by time to the perfect and practical pared down classic forms; mountains of straightforward bowls and dishes transformed by an easy virtuoso paintbrush into a bravura pastiche of the sort of stuff that sits trapped elsewhere in museum cases.

POT PARADE
Opposite above left Mysterious Peruvian containers in sculptural shapes.
Opposite above right Green glaze dripped onto cream in typical Majorcan highly glazed pots.
Opposite below left One of the charms of terracotta is that it will do what you want it to, within limits. If your culinary fetishes require a tall, two-part vessel with a spigot-hole at the bottom, the clay will oblige with finesse.
Opposite below right Strong Indian colours in a simple shape from Santa Fe.

FAKE FRUIT
Above A basket of brightly coloured pottery fruit, the like of which embellishes a *trompe l'oeil* still life on the wall of Frida Kahlo's house. Decorative pieces of fruit can be made from wood and painted. Alternatively, papier mâché is easy to use. It is inexpensive and does not require expert techniques.

NATURAL GOOD TASTE
Opposite far left **The simplest ingredients, transformed by Thai artisans into object lessons in elegance. Here unglazed earthenware pots are arranged with the complementary materials of wood and cane.**

PAINTED BOWL
Opposite above right **An underglaze of dots and flowers adorns this beautiful antique bowl from Marrakesh.**

PITHOI ANSWERS
Opposite below right **A handsome Cretan pithos makes a good contrast with the rough hewn stone.**

ETRUSCAN COLOURS
Below **A nutbrown still life of painted terracotta and venerable carved wood is both elegant and ethnic. A wooden platter incorporates a pale, etched design and is combined with interestingly-shaped urns that are useful and decorative.**

GLOSSARY

ADINKRA Asante cloth printed in blocks of symbolic design, usually in black on brown, white or primary colours.

ADIRE ELEKO Yoruba cloth, stencilled or freehand resist patterned with cassava paste and dyed indigo.

ADOBE Unbaked sundried earth bricks.

ALICATADOS Small geometric shaped tiles in repeating patterns, or a mosaic of fragments of tiles set in plaster. Islamic, and beautifully displayed in the Alhambra Palace, Granada.

AMISH A religious community based in Pennsylvania, espoused to the virtues of plainness and simplicity. They make beautiful artefacts of Shaker severity, and stunning patchwork quilts in strong plain colours.

APPALACHIAN Rustic twig furniture from the Appalachian mountains in the United States.

ARMOIRE Large cupboard, often painted.

AZULEJOS Geometric tiles, larger than alicatados, produced in 16th-century Spain. Also a Portuguese term for decorative wall tiles.

BANGLA A single-storey country house in India, the precedent for the much maligned bungalow.

BARGEBOARD A board, often ornamental, running along the edge of a gable.

BEVEL To trim a piece of timber so that it slants at an angle. A precise 45 degree angle is known as a 'chamfer'.

CASEIN PAINT 18th- and 19th-century paints bound with buttermilk. Suprisingly hardwearing, matt, and ages elegantly.

CAST IRON Ironwork shaped by pouring while molten into a mould.

CERULEAN The colour of cloudless blue sky.

CHAMPLEVE TILES Literally 'raised field': a method of enamelling reminiscent of cloisonné, called cuenca when applied to tiles.

CHARPOY Light transportable Indian bedstead.

CHEVRON A zigzag ornament, like those around the doorways of Norman churches.

COCHINEAL A carmine dye made from the dried bodies of the cactus beatle, *coccus cacti*.

COLOURWASHING Translucent lively paint finish, using layers of thin water-based paint, patchily applied.

CRACKLEGLAZE Decorative finish to simulate the fine cracks of antique oriental ceramics, produced by using two varnishes with different bases.

CUENCA Spanish method of producing three-dimensional tiles in a mould (like encaustic tiles), in which coloured glazes separated by the raised sections depict geometric or plant motifs.

CURLICUE A fantastic curl or twist.

DACHA Russian country house, from wooden cabin upwards.

DELFTWARE Tin-glazed earthenware wall tiles, often white with a bucolic scene hand-painted in blue, originating with the Dutch in the early 17th century.

DHARANIYO Large embroidered and appliquéd cloth used as a hanging in front of a pile of quilts, in Kutch and Saurashtra.

DHURRIE Indian cotton flatweave carpet, rectangular and fringed and used for curtains and sofa-covers as well as floors.

DISTEMPER Whiting or other pigments mixed with size and water and used as paint, particularly for ceilings. Supplanted by emulsion paint.

DISTRESS To fake great age in a material, by scratching, sanding, denting, chipping or staining.

EARTH COLOURS Pigments made from clays and materials taken from the ground.

FANLIGHT Glazed decorative window above a door, often fan-shaped.

FILIGREE Delicate carved stone or wood, as fine as jewellery.

FALUN RED Typical Scandinavian rust-red exterior paint for wooden houses.

FRETWORK Carved woodwork in decorative patterns cut with a fretsaw.

GANESH Hindu elephant-headed god – the remover of obstacles.

GESSO Plaster of Paris, chalk or gypsum, bound with rabbit-skin glue used as a dense smooth white base in painting and mouldings.

GILDING Cover with a fine layer of gold, applied with gold-leaf and sticky gold-size or using commercial gilt paste or wax.

HAVELI Grand mansion of merchant or landlord in western India.

HOPI Southwest American Indians from Arizona and New Mexico, who make, among other things, brilliant and refined wicker baskets.

JAPANESE LACQUER A durable high-gloss finish made up of many layers of pigmented varnish on wood sometimes inlaid with mother-of-pearl or metal.

KELIM Flatwoven tapestry rug, usually in bright geometric designs, from the Middle East.

KOTWAS Strongly decorated appliquéd cloth from Bihar.

LIMEWASH Slaked lime and water as paint for exterior walls.

LIMING Open-grained bare wood finished with liming wax to give it a streaky pallor.

LINOLEUM Floor covering made by coating canvas with a preparation of oxidized linseed oil.

LINSEED OIL Oil extracted from flax seeds and used as the binder in artists' oil-paints, and the main constituents of glazes.

LINTEL A horizontal piece of timber or stone placed over a door or window to bear the weight of the wall above.

MAIOLICA Richly painted ceramics with bright colours on a white ground originating in Renaissance Italy.

MATSURI Japanese festivals – there are 250 celebrated annually in Tokyo alone.

NAVAJO Southwest American Indians, skilled at weaving and the source of bright rugs of a strong geometric design – these days usually in black, red, yellow, indigo and white.

NICHE Wall recess for a religious icon, statue, bust or shelves.

ORPIMENT A bright yellow mineral, yellow arsenic, used as a pigment to which the name King's Yellow is given.

PACHITPATI Gujarati embroidered frieze to be hung above a doorway or beneath a shelf.

PANTORAN Patched and embroidered Kutch wallhangings intended to bring good fortune.

PARGETING A method of adorning the outside of (usually East Anglian) buildings with decorative relief or intaglio plasterwork.

PEDIMENT A low gable, often classical Greek inspired and triangular or semi-circular, placed over niches, doors or windows.

PILASTER Square or rectangular column or pillar attached to a wall, decorative rather than structural.

PISE-DE-TERRE Stiff clay or earth kneaded or mixed with gravel and used as a building material in parts of France, China, England and Africa. Layers are hardened and dried *in situ* between shuttering boards.

QUARRY TILES Unglazed burnt clay nonporous tiles.

QUOIN External angle of the wall of a building – a cornerstone.

RAG RUGS The thrifty expedient familiar to country people in America, Scandinavia, and England, of recycling worn out clothes and blankets in the form of knotted, woven or plaited rugs.

RAS MANDEL Indian embroidered wedding canopy.

ROSMALNING 'Rose painting' – exuberant Norwegian painted peasant furniture.

RYIJI, or RYA RUGS Flat tapestry carpets from Norway and Finland, similar to kelims.

SANKHIA L-shaped embroidered hangings used to decorate doorways on ceremonial occasions, in Saurashtra.

STUGA Scandinavian wooden country cottage or cabin with built-in box beds and bright textiles on wooden walls.

TORAN Gujurati frieze hanging for a doorway, usually richly embroidered with auspicious symbols, and hung with pennants.

VERNACULAR STYLE Unpretentious building style using local materials and familiar design.

WHITING Crushed chalk, used as a pigment or for texture.

WROUGHT IRON Ironwork made by a blacksmith using white-hot forged metal. Usually in strips which require bolting together.

XYSTUS Roman. An open colonnade or walkway planted with trees for recreation and conversation.

FURTHER READING

ARTS AND CRAFTS OF MEXICO Chloe Sayer, Thames and Hudson

NORTH AMERICAN INDIAN ARTS Andrew Hunter Whiteford, Golden Press New York, 1973

AFRICAN TRADITIONAL ARCHITECTURE Susan Denyer, Heinemann, 1978

DOWN TO EARTH MUD ARCHITECTURE: AN OLD IDEA, A NEW FUTURE Jean Dethier, Thames and Hudson, 1981

ART FROM MANY HANDS Jo Miles Schuman, Prentice-Hall, 1981

THE CHINESE HOUSE Ronald G. Knapp, Oxford University Press, 1990

THE SPIRIT OF FOLK ART Henry N. Abrams, New York Insight Guides

TEXTILES ARTS Singer and Spyrou, Black

HUNGARY Gyula Fekete, Corvina

AFRICAN TEXTILES John Picton and John Mack, British Museum Publications

TRADITIONAL INDIAN TEXTILES John Gillow and Nicholas Barnard, Thames and Hudson, 1991

GUATEMALA RAINBOW Photos by Gianni Vecchiato, Pomegranate

EMBROIDERED TEXTILES Sheila Paine, Thames and Hudson, 1990

AEGEAN CROSSROADS James Trilling, The Textile Museum (Washington), 1983

THE HOUSE RESTORER'S GUIDE Hugh Lander, David and Charles

JAPANESE HOMES AND THEIR SURROUNDINGS Edward S. Morse, Dover, 1961

PEOPLES OF THE GOLDEN TRIANGLE Paul and Elaine Lewis, Thames and Hudson

IN THE ORIENTAL STYLE Michael Freeman, Sian Evans, Mimi Lipton, Thames and Hudson

INDEX

Italic numbers show pages on which picture captions occur

Acknowledgments

The publisher thanks the following photographers and organizations for their kind permission to reproduce the photographs in this book:

1 Godeaut/Stylograph; 4–5 Saharoff/Stylograph; 6–7 Kari Haavisto; 10 Kari Haavisto; 12 Guy Bouchet/ Conran Octopus; 13 Simo Rista/J.B.Visual Press; 14 Dirand/Stylograph; 15 Guy Bouchet/Conran Octopus; 16 PIX; 17 Guy Bouchet; 18 Kari Haavisto; 19 above Jean Paul-Bonhommet; 19 below Design Press; 20 above IPC Magazines/WPN; 20 below Christian Sarramon; 21 Bent Rej; 22 Fritz von der Schulenburg (Chiquita Astor); 23 Christian Sarramon; 24 left and above right Jean-Paul Bonhommet; 24 below right Antonio Girbes; 24–5 Bent Rej; 26 Godeaut/ Stylograph; 28 Robert O'Dea; 28–9 James Morris; 30–1 Jean-Pierre Godeaut (Bill Willis); 31 right Carol Beckwith/Robert Estall; 32 Jean-Pierre Godeaut (Jacqueline Foissac); 33 right James Morris; 33 left Jean-Pierre Godeaut (Bill Willis); 34–5 Paul Changuion; 36–7 Margaret Courtney-Clarke; 38 David Massey; 40 above right Jacqui Hurst; 40 below left Carlos Navajas; 40 above left and below right Christian Sarramon; 41 above Jacqui Hurst; 41 below Carlos Navajas; 42 left Anne Garde; 42–3 Jacqui Hurst; 44 Christian Sarramon; 45 David Massey; 46 Marais/ Gaussen/Stylograph; 48 Michael Freeman; 49 Richard Bryant/Arcaid (designers: Gale & Prior); 50 left Michael Freeman; 50–1 Tim Street-Porter/Elizabeth Whiting and Associates; 52 Michael Freeman; 53 Robert Tixador/Agence Top; 54 Michael Boys/Boys Syndication; 54–5 Michael Freeman; 56 left Vogue Living/George Seper; 56–7 Neil Lorimer/Elizabeth Whiting and Associates; 57 above Vogue Living/Rodney Weidland; 57 below Vogue Living/Raffaelle Origone (Painting by Ray Crooke); 58–59 Clive Frost; 60 La Maison de Marie Claire/Sarramon/Roquette; 62 above Brackrock/Stylograph; 62 below Richard Bryant/ Arcaid; 63 Brackrock/Stylograph; 64 above Richard Bryant/Arcaid; 64 below Michael Freeman; 65 Michael Freeman; 66 Bent Rej; 67 Christopher Speakman; 68–9 Christian Sarramon; 70 left Tim Street-Porter/Elizabeth Whiting and Associates; 70–1 Evelyn Hofer; 71 below right Tim Street-Porter/Elizabeth Whiting and Associates; 72 left Horst Neumann/J.B.Visual press; 72–3 La Maison de Marie Claire/Korniloff/Hourdin; 73 right La Maison de Marie Claire/Sarramon/ Sarramon; 74–5 David Black Oriental Carpets; 78 Design Press; 80 above Richard Bryant/Arcaid (designers: Gale & Prior); 80 below Michael Freeman; 81 Design Press; 82 left David Phelps; 82 right James Morris; 83 left Roy/Explorer; 83 right Christian Sarramon; 85 Derry Moore; 86 left and above right James Morris; 86 below right Jean-Pierre Godeaut; 87 above James Morris; 87 below Michael Boys/Boys Syndication; 88 above left Yves Duronsoy; 88 centre left Guy Bouchet; 88 below left Paul Ryan/J.B.Visual Press; 88–9 Bent Rej; 89 right Tim Street-Porter/ Elizabeth Whiting and Associates; 90 left Tim Street-Porter/Elizabeth Whiting and Associates; 90–1 John Hall; 91 right Tim Street-Porter/Elizabeth Whiting and Associates; 92 Michael Freeman; 94 Derry Moore; 95 La Maison de Marie Claire/Beaufre/Billaud; 96 Tim Street-Porter/Elizabeth Whiting and Associates; 97 Gilles de Chabaneix; 98 James Morris; 100 above Paul Changuion; 100 below Fritz von der Schulenburg (F. Miani D'Angoris); 101 Christian Sarramon; 102 Tim Street-Porter/Elizabeth Whiting and Associates; 103 Carlos Navajas; 104 above Bent Rej; 104 below Guy Bouchet; 104–5 Ianthe Ruthven; 106 Carlos Navajas; 108 Paul Changuion; 109 above left Raphael del Vecchio/PIX; 109 above right Carlos Navajas; 109 below left Yves Duronsoy; 109 below right C.Wolff/ Explorer; 110 Design Press; 111 left Raphael del Vecchio/PIX; 111 right Carlos Navajas; 112–3 above F. Peuriot/PIX; 112–3 below Simo Rista/J.B.Visual Press; 113 right Paul Ryan/J.B. Visual Press; 114 Michelle Garrett/Insight; 116 above left Michael Boys/ Boys Syndication; 116 above centre David Black Oriental Carpets; 116 above right Montbazet/Explorer; 116 below left Christian Sarramon; 116 below centre Hilary Emberton; 116 below right Michael Freeman; 117 The Alistair Hull Collection; 118 Fritz von der Schulenburg (Gerald Pearce); 119 above left Jean-Pierre Godeaut (Tami Tazi); 119 above right David Massey; 119 below Christian Sarramon; 120 above Jean-Pierre Godeaut (Major Andersen Le Caire); 120 below Tim Street-Porter/Elizabeth Whiting and Associates; 121 Jean-Pierre Godeaut (Tami Tazi); 122 Richard Bryant/Arcaid; 123 Bent Rej; 124 La Maison de Marie Clarie/Chabaneix/Rozensztroch; 125 left Derry Moore; 125 above right James Morris; 125 below right Clay Perry; 126 Noelle Hoeppe; 128 above left Jean-Pierre Godeaut; 128 above right David Massey; 128 below left Michael Freeman; 128 below right James Morris; 129 Godeaut/Stylograph; 130 above Christian Sarramon; 130 below Godeaut/Stylograph; 130–1 Simo Rista/J.B.Visual Press; 132 above Carlos Navajas; 132 below Christian Sarramon; 133 Andreas von Einsidel/Elizabeth Whiting and Associates; 134 above left Karen Bussolini; 134 above right Christian Sarramon; 134 below left La Maison de Marie Claire/ Dirand; 134 below right Christian Sarramon; 135 Sue Cunningham; 136 left Gilles de Chabaneix; 136 above right Lignon/Stylograph; 136 below right Christian Sarramon; 137 Lignon/Stylograph.

AUTHOR'S ACKNOWLEDGMENTS

It has been pure pleasure writing this book – aside from the subject matter which is a timely celebration of the indomitably jubilant human spirit, the people at Conran Octopus have been a revelation to work with. Jessica Walton found the most elusive pictures with cool competence, Karen Bowen made them cohere – with intelligence and sensitivity – to their mutual advantage, and Jo Bradshaw (with Rod Mackenzie's heroic assistance) managed a virtuoso juggling act with a kaleidoscope of bits and pieces, and effected the difficult marriage of words and images. I would also like to thank Deidre McSharry for her continuing inspiration, Francine Lawrence for her exceptional generosity, my family for their patience, and my mother for dragging her children around the world at an impressionable age.